Close
Reading
Non-Fiction 11–14

Close Reading
Non-Fiction 11–14

Comprehension, Interpretation and
Language Activities

Mary M Firth
Andrew G Ralston

Illustrations by
Moira Munro

Hodder Gibson

A MEMBER OF THE HODDER HEADLINE GROUP

The Publishers would like to thank the following for permission to reproduce copyright material:

Photo credits
Vaughn Youtz/Zuma/Corbis (page 7); Aladin Abdel Naby/Reuters/Corbis (page 11); Bettmann/Corbis (pages 16, 32, 65, 78); ffoto fictions/Alamy (page 25); Cristina Pedrazzini/Science Photo Library (page 26); Reuters/Corbis (page 37); Doug Houghton/Alamy (page 42); Johannes Denysschen/Alamy (page 48); Tony Kyriacou/Rex Features (page 52); Mark Clarke/Science Photo Library (page 53); Rex Features (page 59); Hulton-Deutsch Collection/Corbis (page 71); LWA-Dann Tardif/Corbis (page 72); 1989 Roger Ressmeyer/NASA/Corbis (page 83).

Acknowledgements
pp.7–8 extract from *Radical Sports: Skateboarding* by Andy Horsley © 2002 Heinemann Library; pp.11–12 extract from *Hidden World Series: The Egyptians and the Valley of the Kings* by Philip Steele © 1994 Zoë Books Ltd; pp.16–17 extract from *The Short and Bloody History of Spies* by John Farman © 2000 Random House Children's books; pp.21–22 extract from *Coping with Parents* by Peter Corey © 1989 Peter Corey; pp.26–27 extract from *What's the Big Idea? Food* by Emily Moore © Hodder Children's books (1999); pp.32–33 extract from *John Lennon: Voice of a Generation* by Liz Gogerly © 2002 Hodder Wayland; pp.37–38 extract from *The Olympic Spirit* by Norman Barrett © 1995 Wayland (Publishers) Ltd; pp.42–44 extract from *Picts* by Anna Ritchie © 1989 Crown Copyright; pp.48–49 extract from 'No-frills £89m boost for Scotland' from *Airport News (Pik-Up)*; pp.53–55 extract from 'Cutting Spam out of your Mobile Diet' by Emma Clark © 14 Feb 2002, from BBC News at bbcnews.com; pp.59–60 extract from *Racism* by Adrian Cooper © 2002 Harcourt Education Ltd; pp.65–66 extract from *Great Olympic Moments* by Haydn Middleton © 1999 Reed Educational and Professional Publishing Ltd; pp.72–74 extract from 'Why It's Right to be a Leftie' by Michael Hanlon, 9 March 2002 © The *Daily Mail*; pp.77–78 extract from *Life in the Age of Exploration* by Christopher Falkus © 1994 The Readers Digest Association Limited; pp.82–84 extract from 'Yes, There is Life Out There' by Michael Hanlon, 1 April 2004 © The *Daily Mail*.

Every effort has been made to trace all copyright holders, but if any have been inadvertently overlooked the Publishers will be pleased to make the necessary arrangements at the first opportunity.

Although every effort has been made to ensure that website addresses are correct at time of going to press, Hodder Gibson cannot be held responsible for the content of any website mentioned in this book. It is sometimes possible to find a relocated web page by typing in the address of the home page for a website in the URL window of your browser.

Papers used in this book are natural, renewable and recyclable products. They are made from wood grown in sustainable forests. The logging and manufacturing processes conform to the environmental regulations of the country of origin.

Orders: please contact Bookpoint Ltd, 130 Milton Park, Abingdon, Oxon OX14 4SB. Telephone: (44) 01235 827720. Fax: (44) 01235 400454. Lines are open from 9.00 – 6.00, Monday to Saturday, with a 24-hour message answering service. Visit our website at www.hoddereducation.co.uk. Hodder Gibson can be contacted direct on: Tel: 0141 848 1609; Fax: 0141 889 6315; email: hoddergibson@hodder.co.uk

© 2005 Mary M Firth, Andrew G Ralston
First published in 2005 by
Hodder Gibson, a member of the Hodder Headline Group
2a Christie Street
Paisley PA1 1NB

ISBN 10: 0340 889 225
ISBN 13: 9780 340 889 220

Impression number	10 9 8 7 6 5 4 3 2
Year	2010 2009 2008 2007 2006 2005

ISBN 10: 0340 889 233 (with answers)
ISBN 13: 9780 340 889 237

Impression number	10 9 8 7 6 5 4 3 2
Year	2010 2009 2008 2007 2006 2005

Typeset by Fakenham Photosetting Limited, Fakenham, Norfolk.
Printed and bound in Great Britain by Martins The Printers, Berwick-upon-Tweed

Illustrations © Moira Munro 2005

A catalogue record for this title is available from the British Library

Contents

Getting Started

Remember the two golden rules that must be followed in all Close Reading answers:

★ Use your own words (unless you are asked to QUOTE).
★ Observe the number of marks for the question.

If you must *always* use your own words, why do only *some* questions include the instruction to answer 'in your own words'?

It is good practice always to use your own words, *unless* you are asked to QUOTE. However, the instruction is deliberately included in those questions where it is particularly likely you might be tempted to 'lift' an answer straight from the text. Remember that such a 'lift' would gain NO marks.

I'm still not sure whether I'm writing the right amount for each question. Sometimes I get full marks when I write a short answer, and other times I get half-marks or fewer for a long answer!

The reason for this is that the marker will have a 'marking scheme'. In a 2-mark question, for example, the marker may be looking for two basic points in your answer. If you have stated these briefly but clearly, you will get full marks. In a longer answer which gains fewer marks, you may have failed to make an important point, or merely repeated yourself.

However, you should aim to write answers that are **in proportion**.

Let's suppose the first three questions in a test are for 2, 2 and 4 marks, in that order. Which of these answer patterns is most likely to gain full marks?

1
sds fjdgnjgn jfg nfn fjkhn knhgfnh kjfsn hbfnhfdnhkfdnmhk sfnhfn ghgfhjgfjhg hnfhsnfhknfdkhnf dkhsn fshjksgkhsgm kjhkmlkfnklg

2
sds fjdgnjgn jfg nfn fjkhn knhgfnh kjfsn hbfnhfdnhkfdnmhk sfnhfn

3
sds fjdgnjgn jfg nfn fjkhn knhgfnh kjfsn hbfnhfdnhkfdnmhk sfnhfn

Pattern 1

1
sds fjdgnjgn jfg nfn fjkhn knhgfnh kjfsn hbfnhfdnhkfdnmhk sfnhfn

2
sds fjdgnjgn jfg nfn fjkhn knhgfnh kjfsn hbfnhfdnhkfdnmhk sfnhfn ghgfhjgfjhg hnfhsnfhknfdkhnf dkhsn fshjksgkhsgm kjhkmlkfnklg

3
sds fjdgnjgn jfg nfn fjkhn knhgfnh kjfsn hbfnhfdnhkfdnmhk sfnhfn

Pattern 2

1
sds fjdgnjgn jfg nfn fjkhn knhgfnh kjfsn hbfnhfdnhkfdnmhk sfnhfn

2
sds fjdgnjgn jfg nfn fjkhn knhgfnh kjfsn hbfnhfdnhkfdnmhk sfnhfn

3
sds fjdgnjgn jfg nfn fjkhn knhgfnh kjfsn hbfnhfdnhkfdnmhk sfnhfn ghgfhjgfjhg hnfhsnfhknfdkhnf dkhsn fshjksgkhsgm kjhkmlkfnklg

Pattern 3

The answer is pattern 3. Since question 3 is worth double the marks of questions 1 and 2, you should write roughly *double* the number of words.

What will the questions in these tests be looking for?

★ Your understanding of the facts.
★ Your appreciation of the writer's expression.
★ Your thoughts on some of the issues.

Why do some questions have subsections, in the form of 1a) and 1b), instead of being asked separately (1, 2, 3, etc.)?

When a question has subsections, these will be on a related point, or deal with the same part of the text.

Must I write in sentences? Can I save time and use bullet points?

Write in sentences if you need to explain something, such as an effect of style. But try to make them as brief as possible – you do *not* need to repeat the words of the question.

Bullet points are acceptable in answers which require you to give facts. Bullet points are dots followed by brief notes, written one below the other. They are a good idea in summary questions. For example, if you were asked to summarise facts for 4 marks about the athlete described in Chapter 12, you could set it out as follows:

Write a **dot** (bullet), followed by a brief note. For example,

● Zatopek was an officer in the Czech army.
● He was 30 years old in 1952.
● His wife Dana was also an Olympic gold medallist.
● He won three gold medals in athletics events in 1952.

As you will see, this gives a very clear format, which is easy for markers to follow. The marker can see instantly that you have provided four separate points. Many examination boards now encourage the use of bullet-point answers, particularly in summary-type questions.

Is there anything I need to know before I answer these questions?

You will need to know:

1 Four **figures of speech**:

★ simile (a comparison using 'like' or 'as')
★ metaphor (a comparison where one thing is said to *be* another)
★ alliteration (deliberate repetition of initial letters of words in a phrase)
★ personification (a comparison of an object to a person).

2 The term '**tone**'.

Tone refers to the way writers reveal their attitude to a subject. For example, they might adopt a tone that is humorous, ironic, dramatic or chatty.

3 The term '**sentence structure**'.

This refers to the way a sentence is composed and the way the words and phrases in a sentence are arranged. Sentences may be simple or complex, long or short. **Inversion** is the name given to a technique where the normal word order is turned around to emphasise a particular part of the sentence. For example, an important element might be put at the beginning for impact.

Punctuation is a good guide to sentence structure. A full stop, question mark or exclamation mark will indicate the type of sentence, while commas separate phrases and clauses or indicate a list. This book will explain more complex marks, such as colons, semicolons, dashes and brackets.

What should I say in 'word choice' questions?

As the wording implies, you will be asked to explain the effect of the writer's choice of words.

In the case of a question that directs you to a particular word or phrase, a good approach is to think of a simpler word or expression the writer could have chosen, and then consider what difference is made by the one he or she *did* choose.

If you are asked to comment on 'word choice' more generally, be sure to **quote** examples, and discuss each one individually. One example for every mark available is about right.

DO	DON'T
Skim-read the passage first.	Read the passage through twice before answering the questions as many old-fashioned books recommended.
Re-read more carefully section by section.	
Keep your answers in proportion to the marks: write *more* for questions that are worth a lot of marks.	Spend too long on 1-mark questions.
QUOTE examples in questions on style and word choice.	'Lift' answers straight from the text unless you are asked to QUOTE.
Discuss each of the examples you quote in style questions *individually*.	Lump examples together with a vague general comment in your answers to word-choice questions.

Chapter 1

Skateboarding

In recent years there has been a huge increase in the popularity of skateboarding, particularly among 12 to 14-year-olds.

Extract

1

5

Skateboarding began in the late 1950s on the West Coast of America, where a group of bored Californian surfers tried putting a surfboard on rollerskate wheels.

The earliest skateboards were very crude and dangerous forms of transport. The main problem was their rattling steel wheels, which made the skateboard shake. The steel wheels were soon replaced by ones made of baked clay, and eventually in the early 1970s by the smooth urethane plastic that is still used today.

The board shape stayed similar to the miniature wooden surfboard that it was modelled on. These 'old school' boards were made from wood, plastic or even metal and were designed to be cruised on. The introduction of the kicktail – an upturned back end – in the late 1960s allowed new tricks to be invented. There were many changes in board shape throughout the 1970s and 1980s. Most modern boards are made from maple wood and have both a kicktail and an upturned nose.

The two main types of skateboarding are street and ramp. Street skating is skateboarding using urban obstacles such as

10

15

20

25

Extract continued

Did you know ...?

How many skateboarders are there in the USA?

30   a) 1 million
b) 10 million
c) 100 million

(The correct answer is on Page 9.)

35

kerbs, stairs and handrails. This can be dangerous and is banned in some cities. However, many skateparks have streetcourses that copy the urban landscape. Skateparks offer a safe place to practise and can introduce you to ramp skating. These are also known as halfpipes, and are shaped like a letter 'U'. Ramps come in three main sizes – mini, midi and vert, which is vertical at the top.

Once you've stepped on a skateboard you'll understand why so many people love it. It holds many challenges and is constantly fun and exciting. As you begin to perfect tricks you
40   will become more and more addicted to this fun pastime.

Taking a closer look ...

Look at paragraph one (lines 1 to 6).

1 Explain in your own words how skateboarding began.   *(2 marks)*

Look at paragraph two (lines 7 to 15).

2 Explain in your own words why the earliest skateboards were dangerous.   *(2 marks)*

3 Name TWO different materials that have been used to make wheels for skateboards.   *(2 marks)*

Look at paragraph three (lines 16 to 23).

4 a)   What change took place to the shape of the skateboard in the 1960s?   *(2 marks)*

   b)   In your own words, explain the effect this had on skateboarding.   *(2 marks)*

5 Describe the features of a modern skateboard.   *(2 marks)*

Look at paragraph four (lines 24 to 36).

6 What are the two main types of skateboarding? *(2 marks)*

7 Describe what the first of these types involves. *(2 marks)*

8 Skateboarders might not like being banned by cities. In your own words, explain ONE reason why the ban should be accepted as fair. *(2 marks)*

Look at paragraph five (lines 37 to 40).

9 Clearly the writer is enthusiastic about skateboarding. Quote FOUR different words that suggest this. *(2 marks)*

TOTAL MARKS: 20

('Did you know?' answer: b)

Focus on language

Jargon

The writer of this passage uses a number of words like 'kicktail' and 'halfpipe' which are familiar to those who know about skateboarding but are not generally used in everyday conversation.

Words of this kind are known as **jargon** – technical terms connected with a particular subject area or job.

Other jargon words connected with skateboarding are 'grind', 'quarterpipe' and 'slamming'.

Think of five examples of jargon words used in each of the following areas:

★ medicine
★ cars
★ football
★ mathematics
★ another subject area, sport or special interest that you know about in some depth.

Looking at the issues

➤ *In the USA over 80,000 people per year require emergency hospital treatment for injuries caused by skateboarding.*
➤ *One third of skateboard injuries are suffered by skateboarders who have been skating for less than a week.*
➤ *Wearing pads can reduce wrist and elbow injuries by about 85 per cent.*

Bearing these facts in mind, discuss what could be done to make skateboarding safer.

Ideas for writing

★ Describe the scene at a busy skateboarding park (without telling a story).

★ Write a story in which a skateboarding competition is a central element.

★ Write a letter to a friend, recommending skateboarding as a hobby. Explain your reasons clearly.

Chapter 2

The Living Dead

The ancient Egyptians believed that it was very important to preserve (mummify) the bodies of their rulers (called pharaohs) because they thought that their bodies survived in the afterlife . . .

Extract

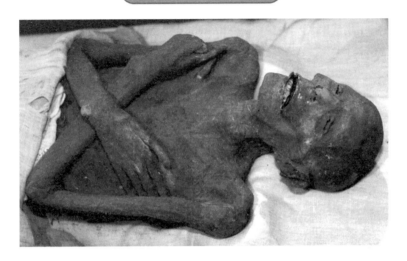

1   Archaeologists can find out a great deal from the way in which people are buried. Normally they only find skeletons, but sometimes bodies are preserved naturally. This has happened in the bogs and marshes of northern Europe and in the deep-frozen
5   soil of Siberia. Bodies buried in dry desert sands are particularly well-preserved. The secret of preparing mummies was also discovered in other desert regions of the world, such as Peru.

The Egyptians were fascinated by death. The west bank of Thebes is sometimes called a necropolis. This Greek word means
10   'city of the dead'. The Egyptians learned how to prepare mummies as early as 4000 BC. Preserving dead bodies, or embalming, was important to them because they believed that their bodies survived into the next life. The citizens of Thebes

> **Extract continued**

even mummified sacred animals such as cats and crocodiles. Poor
15 people were embalmed, but the best treatment was given to those
who could pay for it – royalty, nobles and priests.

Often the brain was the first organ to be removed from the
dead body. The heart was left in place, but the kidneys, liver,
stomach and guts were taken out and preserved separately. They
20 were placed in jars in the tomb. The body itself was dried out
with natron – a preparation of salty crystals. This process took
about forty days. The body was then stuffed with clay, sawdust or
linen cloth soaked with resin. The skin was rubbed with oils,
scents and wax. Finally, bandages and cloth were wrapped around
25 the body.

The mummies were placed inside a series of wooden coffin
cases. These were shaped like a human body and painted with the
face of the dead person. The coffins were then lowered into a
stone box called a sarcophagus.

Taking a closer look ...

1 Explain why 'The Living Dead' is a good title for this passage.
(2 marks)

2 '[Sometimes] bodies are preserved naturally.' (line 3)
In what THREE natural environments is this most likely to happen?
Base your answer on paragraph one (lines 1–7).   *(3 marks)*

3 Why did the Egyptians think it was important to preserve the
bodies of the dead?   *(2 marks)*

4 a) How was this process taken further in the city of Thebes?

(2 marks)

   b) What word in paragraph two shows the writer thinks that the
Thebans' practices were peculiar?   *(1 mark)*

5 We are told that 'the best treatment was given to those who could
pay for it' (lines 15–16). Give TWO reasons why the process would
be very expensive.   *(2 marks)*

6 Paragraph three (lines 17–25) describes the method of mummification in detail.
   a) What was done with the kidneys, liver, stomach and guts?
   b) What was natron used for?
   c) How long did the body take to dry out?
   d) What materials were used to stuff the body?
   e) How was the skin preserved?
   f) What was the final stage?   (6 marks)

7 Look at lines 26–29. In your own words, describe the wooden coffins in which the mummies were placed.   (2 marks)

TOTAL: 20 MARKS

Focus on language (1)

Dictionary work

Find a word from the passage that means:

a) city of the dead

b) preserving dead bodies

c) an elaborate stone coffin

d) a preparation of salty crystals

Focus on language (2)

Paragraphs

A paragraph is a collection of sentences that are all to do with the same subject.

In writing that deals mostly with facts and information, like 'The Living Dead' passage, a paragraph will often begin with a **topic sentence**, which introduces the topic and is developed in more detail in the rest of the paragraph.

For example, paragraph two begins by saying:

> The Egyptians were fascinated by death.

This point is expanded in the rest of the paragraph, which describes how the Egyptians went to great lengths to preserve the bodies of people and certain animals.

For practice

1 Read the following paragraph.

> The Egyptians believed in many different gods. There was Ra, the sun god, and Osiris, the god of death, for example. Many of their gods were connected with animals, like Horus the falcon-god and Anubis the jackal.

What is the connection between the first sentence and the rest of the paragraph?

2 Use the following topic sentences to begin a paragraph of your own. (Write a paragraph of about six lines in which you expand on the point in the topic sentence.)

a) One incident in my time at primary school will always stay in my mind.

b) Before setting off on a trip abroad, there are several things that a holidaymaker has to do.

Ideas for writing

Using the internet, or resources in your school library, find out more about Howard Carter, Lord Carnarvon, the excavation of Tutankhamen's tomb and 'the curse of the Mummy'.

The story might give you some ideas for writing of your own. Here are some suggestions:

★ Retell the story in a dramatic way, aiming to create suspense and tension. Use some direct speech – that is, make the characters talk for themselves.

★ Is 'the curse of the mummy' simply a superstition or should it be taken seriously? Write a factual, argumentative essay in which you look at the arguments on both sides and reach a conclusion of your own.

★ Use the inscription from the tomb quoted below ('Death Shall Come on Swift Wing …') as the opening sentence of a story of your own that involves an Egyptian setting, archaeologists, etc.

THE CURSE OF THE MUMMY

"Death Shall Come on Swift Wing to Him who

Disturbs

the Peace of the King."

(Inscription said to have been found on Tutankhamen's tomb)

* * *

One of the greatest ever finds in archaeology took place in 1922, when Howard Carter discovered the treasures buried in King Tutankhamen's tomb.

Carter's dig had been financed by Lord Carnarvon. A few months after the tomb was opened, Carnarvon took ill and died in Cairo, probably from an infection caused by an insect bite. Legend has it that, when he died, a power failure occurred in Cairo and all the lights went out. At home in England, Carnarvon's favourite dog suddenly dropped dead.

Some people believed this was 'the curse of the mummy' punishing Carnarvon for disturbing the pharaoh's tomb.

On the other hand, nothing happened to Howard Carter, the man who actually opened up the tomb.

What do *you* think ... ?

Chapter 3

The *Real* James Bond

The character of James Bond was created by Ian Fleming, and since the 1960s the role has been played by famous actors such as Sean Connery, Roger Moore and, most recently, Pierce Brosnan. In writing the stories, Ian Fleming was able to draw on some real-life experiences of his own . . .

Extract

1 You'd never think that the guy who created James Bond knew a lot about real espionage, would you? You'd be wrong. Not only

5 did Ian Fleming (1908–1964) know a lot about it, he'd been in it up to his suave and sophisticated neck for most of his working life – before

10 deciding to write. Not only that, but you might be forgiven for thinking he was a bit like our Mr Bond himself.

Son of wealthy parents, a playboy around London and bored
15 with life as a stockbroker, young Ian craved excitement. He eventually met someone in British Naval Intelligence who was looking for bright young guys who, feeling they had nothing to lose, were prepared to do just about anything as long as it was dangerous and the money was good. Fleming was perfect – mad
20 as a hatter, brave as a bulldog – and with ideas galore.

Fleming's first solo job during the second World War was for Room 39 (as his department was nicknamed) and involved the famous Rudolf Hess (Hitler's deputy leader of the German

Extract continued

National Socialists). He reckoned that if he could get one of the
25 Nazis' top men to defect to us, it would strike pure fear into the
Germans. He chose the infamous Hess purely because of his one
weakness. He was deeply into astrology (star signs) and could be
led to believe almost anything. Fleming managed to get at the
two Swiss astrologers known to be used by high-ranking German
30 officers and told them to tell Hess that his big moment of truth
was nigh, and it was him who had been chosen by the fickle
finger of fate to go to England and smoke big pipe of peace with
our Prime Minister. This, without any doubt, would make him the
greatest and most popular man in the whole wide world. In 1941
35 Hess swallowed the bait big time, borrowed a Messerschmitt
fighter and flew it to Scotland where he ordered the somewhat
gobsmacked local police to take him to their leader.

Oh dear! Instead of being delighted, the British Government,
including PM Winston Churchill, saw him as not only an
40 embarrassment but potentially dangerous. They were worried that
he might shine a torch on all the high-up Britons (including the
Duke of Windsor[1]) who'd been having cosy fireside chats with the
top German, Hitler. The government therefore let it be known
that Hess was a total loony and no use to man nor beast. Hess
45 went to jail and stayed there till he died in 1989.

[1] The brother of King George VI and uncle of Queen Elizabeth II.

Taking a closer look ...

1 Read paragraph two (lines 14–20). In your own words, write down
   FOUR facts that we are told about Ian Fleming's background and
   career.   *(4 marks)*

2 Look at lines 16–20. In your own words, explain what kind of
   people the British intelligence wanted to employ.   *(2 marks)*

3 What did the British hope to gain by winning over Rudolf Hess to
   their side during World War II?   *(2 marks)*

4 Look at lines 30–34.
What story did the astrologers tell Hess about his future destiny?
(2 marks)

5 QUOTE the phrase that shows Hess completely believed this story.
(1 mark)

6 QUOTE the phrase that describes the British Government's reaction to the arrival of Hess in this country. *(1 mark)*

7 In your own words, explain what the British Government was worried that Hess might do. *(2 marks)*

8 What did the British Government do with Hess? *(2 marks)*

9 Find a word or phrase in the passage that means:
a) to change your loyalty from one country to another
b) spying in order to find out another country's secrets
c) having an elegant, smooth and cultured manner
d) the belief that the stars and planets influence people's lives.
(4 marks)

TOTAL MARKS: 20

Focus on language

Informal writing

What makes this passage interesting is the way the writer takes a chatty and light-hearted approach to his subject. It is almost as if he is talking directly to us. Various features of the style of the passage give it an **informal** tone:

The writer takes a **personal approach**. Look at the opening sentence, for example.

> You'd never think that the guy who created James Bond knew a lot about real espionage, would you?

Note the use of the personal pronoun 'you'. The sentence takes the form of a question, which also makes it sound more personal, as if he is asking the reader, 'What do *you* think?'

The **word choice** is also conversational. He doesn't always use factual or formal vocabulary:

> *total loony*
> *somewhat gobsmacked*
> *mad as a hatter*

The writer sometimes uses ***alliteration*** (a series of words beginning with the same letter) to create a light-hearted effect:

> The fickle finger of fate.

He uses **exaggeration** to make the story sound more dramatic:

> His moment of truth was nigh.
> This, without any doubt, would make him the greatest and most popular man in the whole wide world.

To understand the effect of these techniques, look at this version of the story of Ian Fleming and Rudolf Hess, which is written in a more formal way:

> The first task Ian Fleming carried out when he worked for British Naval Intelligence was to engineer the defection to Great Britain of Rudolf Hess, the deputy leader of the Nazi Party in Germany. Knowing that Hess was a strong believer in astrology, Fleming arranged for him to be told that his destiny in life was to come to Britain and negotiate peace with the Prime Minister, Winston Churchill. Hess was convinced by this story and fled to Scotland in 1941. However, the government considered his presence in this country to be dangerous and had him imprisoned for the rest of his life.

For practice (1)

(For group discussion or for written answers)

What *similarities* do you notice between this extract and the passage?

What *differences* are there?

For practice (2)

This chapter mentioned three techniques: informal writing, alliteration and exaggeration.

Look back and check that you know what each of these means.

Which of these three techniques is used in the following examples?

1 Hi there! How's it going?

2 That meal was totally inedible!

3 Proper preparation prevents poor performance.

4 Hitler went crazy when he found out that Hess had done a runner.

5 The Maths exam was impossible.

6 Discovering drugs is the road to ruin.

7 A great day out for the kids – and their mums and dads!

8 I'll die of shame if you phone my teacher.

9 I'm thick, but my sister's dead brainy.

10 Drop the dead donkey.

For practice (3)

Find an informal expression from the passage that means much the same as these more formal versions:

FORMAL	INFORMAL
1 Clever young men	
2 plenty of original thoughts	
3 very friendly conversations	
4 likely to behave in an odd or unpredictable way	
5 negotiate an end to war	

Ideas for writing

★ Discuss what makes the James Bond films so popular.

★ Invent a character who is a spy. Write a few opening pages for a spy story of your own.

Chapter 4

The Nagging Parent

Everybody argues with their parents at some point. According to writer Peter Corey, though, the Nagging Parent is a particularly difficult type . . .

Extract

1 *The nature of the beast*

Parents ask questions which they already know the answers to. The Nagging Parent is the past master of this art. Not only the past master, but the present and the future master as well. And
5 mistress, in the case of the Nagging Mum. They seem to spend their entire life questioning your actions, telling you that you shouldn't be doing what you're doing, even if it's the exact opposite of the last thing that you were doing. Confused? That's hardly surprising. Because *surprise* is the Nagging Parent's secret
10 weapon.

Habitat

In bushes, behind doors, under beds. In fact, anywhere that provides a bit of cover. Just when you thought it was safe to sit on

15 the loo ... the Nagging Parent strikes: 'Why are you using so much lavatory paper?' Your life is not your own. You can't go anywhere or do anything without getting nagged.

20 And don't imagine you are safe when your parents are not with you. Because you're not! The thing about Nagging Parents is that they are quite happy to nag *anybody*. It doesn't have to be one of their *own* children. What makes it worse is the fact that this particular breed is very common. And what compounds the problem is the fact that the Nagging Parent, or, to give them their Latin name, *Naggus Tu Deathus*, is a distant cousin of that other difficult type, the Inquisitive Parent. You could be doing

25 something fairly harmless – minor surgery on next door's Manx cat (at least, it's a Manx cat *now*, anyway), and totally unbeknown to you, the local snoop has got you recorded for posterity on their Inquisitive Parent's Surveillance Kit (available from all good health centres). Next thing you know, the Nagging Parent is

30 giving you an earful of Relentless Verbal Porridge.

Appearance

Ah! Here is where the Nagging Parent can be very devious. They look perfectly normal. Well, as normal as any parent ever looks. And, like a chameleon, they have the power to blend with their surroundings.

35 That door could be a parent. That wardrobe could be one. That tallboy definitely is one (but at least he's come out of the closet!).

Out of doors, they don't exactly wear army camouflage gear, but they manage to blend in with the background, as they sneak from bush to bush ready to stop you doing whatever it is you're

40 doing, however harmless. Oh, yes! These are devious animals!

Conversation

This seems to consist mainly of phrases that begin: 'Don't' or 'Stop' as in:

'Don't do that!' or

45 'Stop that!'

'That' is their universal word to cover absolutely anything that you may, or may not, be up to. For, be assured, you don't actually have to be doing the thing you're accused of in order to get nagged.

Taking a closer look ...

1   Why do you think the writer uses a long sentence in lines 5–8?
                                                                    (2 marks)

2   The whole passage depends on one basic comparison: parents are
    compared to animals.

    QUOTE THREE expressions which show how the writer talks about
    Nagging Parents and their behaviour as if he was describing a
    species of animal.   *(3 marks)*

3   Explain why a dash is used in line 25.   *(2 marks)*

4   a)   Throughout the passage the writer gives 'Nagging Parents'
         capital letters. Why do you think he does this?   *(2 marks)*
    b)   Find another example of capital letters being used for a similar
         purpose elsewhere in the passage.   *(1 mark)*

5   Like the passage on 'The *Real* James Bond', this one is written in an
    informal style, where the writer appears to be talking to us. QUOTE
    TWO examples of this style from anywhere in the passage.
                                                              (2 marks)

6   Much of the humour of the passage depends on exaggeration (see
    page 19).
    a)   Quote ONE example of this.   *(1 mark)*
    b)   Explain why you think it is funny.   *(2 marks)*

7   Find a word or phrase from the passage that means:
    a)   to be an expert at something
    b)   to make a problem worse
    c)   surroundings in which an animal lives
    d)   a person who is nosy
    e)   a covering used to hide or disguise something   *(5 marks)*

                                             TOTAL MARKS: 20

Focus on language

Apostrophes (1)

Question 5 asked about the informal language in the passage.

One characteristic of informal or spoken English is the use of
shortened forms. We rarely say 'you are' or 'do not' – we shorten (or
abbreviate) these to 'you're' and 'don't'.

The rule to follow here is:

> The apostrophe goes in the place where the letter has been missed out.

For practice

a) Find FIVE different examples of apostrophes being used in this way in the passage.

Copy them out and then write them in full. For example,

> You shouldn't do that.
>
> shouldn't → should not

(*Note*: don't choose the word 'parent's'. The apostrophe is used for a different purpose here. This will be explained in the next chapter.)

b) Write out the following sentences, changing the underlined words into their shortened forms, using apostrophes.

1 I <u>cannot</u> believe how <u>she has</u> changed since I last saw her.

2 <u>It is</u> not very long since she visited us.

3 <u>You would</u> have said exactly the same thing <u>if you had</u> been there.

4 <u>Do not</u> stand on that wall. <u>You will</u> probably fall off.

5 <u>Let us</u> go into town this weekend. I <u>have not</u> been for ages.

Looking at the issues

For group discussion:

★ How seriously do you think the writer expects us to take this passage?
★ What would happen if parents *didn't* nag their children?
★ How far does the passage describe your view of your own parents? Talk about some of your personal experiences and see if other members of your group have similar stories to relate.

Ideas for writing

American writer Erma Bombeck once said:

> When my kids become wild and unruly, I use a nice, safe playpen. When they're finished, I climb out.

★ Do you think parents are too strict with children or not strict enough?
★ Write a story based on the above quotation.

Diane Loomans, author of a number of books on parenting, wrote:

> If I had my child to raise all over again,
> I'd finger-paint more, and point the finger less.
> I would do less correcting and more connecting.

★ What do you think she meant? Do you agree with her? What makes it difficult for parents to spend time with their children?
★ Write about what *you* think the qualities of a good parent are.

Chapter 5

How Safe is the Food We Eat?

Today we are used to being able to buy food from large supermarkets. Because of this, farming methods are very different from what they used to be, and some of these changes have their disadvantages . . .

Extract

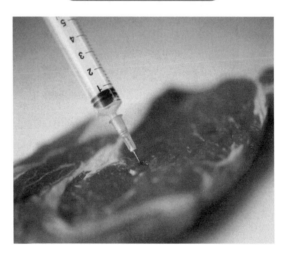

1 Before the war, everyone bought their food from small shops – the bakers, the butchers and the greengrocers. Then in the 1950s large supermarkets started springing up, mainly because fridges had improved and become widely available.

5 We began to eat more and more processed food – food that has had something done to it before we buy it. Supermarkets and processed food are designed to make life easier for people who work long hours and haven't the time to go from shop to shop, or to spend a long time cooking when they get home.

10 Now only 8% of supermarket food is fresh (fruit, veg and eggs); the rest has gone through food company machines. Processing food costs money, but the companies that do it can

charge the consumer more than it cost them, so making big profits.
15 A frozen french fry is far removed from the original (cheap) potato which it's made from.

It's important to watch out and read labels because sometimes
20 low quality food is disguised with flavourings and colours to look and taste fresher and better than it really is.

Over the past few years there have been an alarming number of food scares. Almost all of them are connected to intensive
25 farming.

Animals are being pushed with selective breeding and drugs to produce much more than their bodies were designed to do. A dairy cow used to live an average of fifteen years or more. Modern dairy cows are worn out after only six. Now new technologies and
30 drugs are pushing them to produce even more. But will it end in disaster?

Intensive farming conditions take their toll on animals. They are often given antibiotics and other drugs to keep them healthy enough to produce what we want from them, i.e. milk, eggs and
35 meat. One fear is that humans who eat products made from the flesh or milk of these animals are also eating low dosages of antibiotics. Traces of antibiotics have been found in pork and turkey – there are fears that humans are eating so much that the bacteria inside us are becoming immune to antibiotics.

> **Did you know . . . ?**
>
> In a lifetime the average UK meat eater will eat 36 pigs, 30 sheep, 8 cows and 550 chickens, ducks and turkeys!

Taking a closer look . . .

1 Read paragraph one (lines 1–4). Explain why large supermarkets started to spring up in the 1950s.

(1 mark)

2 a) For what purpose does the writer use a dash in line 1? *(2 marks)*

b) From elsewhere in the passage, find another example of a dash being used for a similar purpose. *(1 mark)*

3 From paragraph two (lines 5–9), state, in your own words, TWO advantages of supermarkets and processed food. *(2 marks)*

4 Read paragraph three (lines 10–17).
   a) What is the disadvantage of supermarket food? *(1 mark)*
   b) How do the food companies make their profits? *(2 marks)*

5 Read paragraph four (lines 18–22). Why is it important to read the labels on food? *(2 marks)*

6 a) What do you think is the purpose of 'selective breeding'? *(2 marks)*
   b) QUOTE another example of jargon similar to 'selective breeding'. *(1 mark)*

7 Read paragraphs five to seven (23–39). Explain the harmful effects of modern farming methods on:
   a) cows *(2 marks)*
   b) humans who eat the food that comes from these animals. *(2 marks)*

8 In Chapter One ('Skateboarding'), we looked at jargon. QUOTE TWO words from the passage above that could be described as examples of medical jargon. *(2 marks)*

TOTAL MARKS: 20

True or false?

	T	F
1 Before the 1950s few people had fridges in their homes.	☐	☐
2 92 per cent of food sold in supermarkets has been processed in some way.	☐	☐
3 Flavourings and colours are used to improve the quality of food.	☐	☐
4 Modern methods of farming help cows to live longer.	☐	☐
5 If animals are given antibiotics, some of these may find their way into the human food chain.	☐	☐

Focus on language

Apostrophes (2)

In Chapter Four we saw how apostrophes can be used to show that a letter has been missed out.

For example, one sentence in the passage refers to 'people who work long hours and haven't the time to go from shop to shop'. Instead of writing 'have not' in full, the writer puts 'haven't'.

An apostrophe can also be used to indicate ownership, as in 'my friend's house'.

Six rules for the use of 'ownership' apostrophes

➤ If the word is singular, put an apostrophe and an 's' after it:

> the baby's pram

➤ If the word is plural and already ends with an 's', put the apostrophe after the 's':

> the girls' team
> the babies' nursery

➤ Some words like *children* and *men* are plural forms but don't end with an 's'. As the word is already plural, simply add an apostrophe and an 's' to show possession:

> the men's room
> the children's playground

It would be wrong to write *childrens'* or *mens'*.

➤ The word *it's* is an exception to these rules. When 'its' is used to indicate ownership, **no** apostrophe is used:

> The car was in its garage.

➤ The only time that *its* has an apostrophe is when it is short for *it is*:

> It's time to go home.

➤ Don't stick in an apostrophe every time you see a word ending with the letter 's'! Only use one if possession is involved.

For practice

a) Rewrite the following sentences, inserting apostrophes as required. Remember: before you insert an apostrophe, ask yourself:

★ Has a letter been missed out?

★ Is ownership involved?

1 You have to put in a £1 coin to use one of the supermarkets trolleys.

2 I dont seem to have any change. You couldnt lend me £1, could you?

3 Its not fair – youre always expecting me to lend you money.

4 This shops prices seem to be much dearer than those in the one across the road.

5 Peoples eating habits have changed over the last fifty years.

6 The new superstore was popular with customers because its car park was very spacious.

7 I prefer to buy meat from the butchers shop rather than from a supermarket.

8 After their classes, the students went to the students union to play snooker.

9 The speakers voice was so quiet that the audience couldnt really make out what he was saying.

10 Its been good fun taking part in the schools drama production but I dont think Ill ever be a professional actor.

b) All of the following sentences contain the word 'its'. Rewrite **only** the ones where there should be an apostrophe ('it's'):

1 A team will always be judged on its results.

2 Its been good to see you again.

3 Something's wrong with my mobile phone – its battery isn't holding the charge.

4 Its important to put the apostrophe in the right place.

5 If you feel sick its maybe because you've eaten so many chocolates.

Looking at the issues

Discuss one or more of the following issues in groups. Your ideas could then be written up in the form of an essay or report.

★ It is sometimes said that young people's diet consists of sweets, crisps, burgers and fizzy drinks! Do you think there is any truth in this view?

★ Are you concerned about what you eat? What changes do you think you should make in your eating habits? How difficult is it to change to a more healthy diet?

★ According to the Vegetarian Society, 7 per cent of the UK adult population is vegetarian. Among 15–24-year-olds, the figure is 12 per cent. Why do you think people become vegetarians? Do you think this is a good idea or not?

★ Statistics indicate that 32 per cent of women and 46 per cent of men in the UK are overweight. What steps do you think people should take to keep fit and healthy?

Chapter 6

Five Shots that Killed John Lennon

The famous 1960s pop group the Beatles consisted of John Lennon, Paul McCartney, George Harrison and Ringo Starr. The group split up in 1970. In 1971 John Lennon moved to New York and never returned to Britain again.

Extract

1　John Lennon had always felt safe in New York. The autograph-hunters were polite and fans didn't bother him. On 5　Monday 8 December 1980 there didn't seem any reason to feel differently. John and his wife Yoko had more interviews with the media than usual, but that 10　was to be expected with the release of 'Double Fantasy'.[1] They had no idea that a young man called Mark Chapman had been tracing their movements 15　for a week.

At about 4pm John signed an autograph for Chapman outside their apartment. John looked up when he'd finished signing and asked, 'Is that all? Do you want anything else?' Chapman later said he felt that John had known he was looking his killer in the 20　eyes. John and Yoko then went to the studio. They arrived home at about 10.52pm. As they approached their apartment block, John saw Chapman hiding in the shadows. As he walked past him, Chapman withdrew a gun and shot John five times in the back. Amazingly, John was still alive. He was rushed to hospital in

　[1] A new album released by John Lennon in 1980.

Extract continued

25 the back of a police car. However, his time had run out, and John was pronounced dead at 11.07pm.

As the news of John's death spread across the world, people struggled to understand Chapman's motives. They also tried to come to terms with the loss of John. Most people who remember
30 that tragic day recall where they were and how they felt. On 14 December 1980, crowds gathered in cities around the world for a day of mourning. At 7pm in the UK and 2pm in New York people observed ten minutes of silence. Throughout the day, radio stations everywhere played John's music.

35 By the end of the year, the single 'Starting Over' and album 'Double Fantasy' were number one in the UK and the USA. 'Imagine' later topped the charts, and has reappeared in the British charts in 1988 and 1999. In 1995/96 the remaining Beatles released three albums of previously unreleased Beatles material.
40 'Real Love' and 'Free as a Bird' were of particular interest as they were recorded by John in the 1970s. Paul, George and Ringo had re-mixed them and added their instruments and vocals. For the first time in over two decades the Beatles had been reunited.

In many ways, John will always be here, in his music, and his
45 words. John would have been happy with that – he'd often said the message was all that mattered.

Taking a closer look . . .

1 Why had John Lennon always felt safe in New York?   *(2 marks)*

2 What evidence is there that Mark Chapman had carefully planned his crime?   *(2 marks)*

3 From information contained in the first two paragraphs (lines 1–26), write an account of what John Lennon and his wife Yoko had been doing on 8 December 1980.   *(3 marks)*

4 Name some of the ways that people paid tribute to John Lennon on 14 December 1980. Base your answer on paragraph three (lines 27–34).   *(2 marks)*

5 What evidence is there that his music remained popular in the 1980s and 1990s? *(2 marks)*

6 What changes had been made to 'Real Love' and 'Free as a Bird'? *(2 marks)*

7 In what sense does the writer consider that John Lennon will 'always be here' (line 44)? *(2 marks)*

8 The passage is written in hindsight – that is, after the events have occurred. QUOTE a statement from paragraph one which shows this. *(2 mark)*

9 Most of the passage takes a very factual approach. QUOTE TWO examples of the writer giving precise details. *(2 marks)*

10 QUOTE an example from anywhere in the passage where the writer expresses his own opinion. *(1 mark)*

(TOTAL MARKS: 20)

Focus on language

Sequencing

This passage is written in **chronological order** – that is, in the order in which things happened. The word 'chronological' comes from the Greek word for time (*chronos*).

For practice

The box, below, contains some key dates in the life of John Lennon, but they are not listed in chronological order.

★ Sort them into the right sequence and write a paragraph entitled 'John Lennon and the Beatles'.
★ You should try to link some of the above points together. Remember to write in proper sentences rather than in note form.

John Lennon: key dates

★ Lived in a working-class area called Penny Lane.
★ Formed a band at school called the Quarry Men.
★ Parents separated when he was four. John was brought up by his sister Mimi and her husband George.
★ Did well at primary school and won a place at Quarry Bank Grammar School.
★ Rebelled against the school's discipline.
★ Born 9 October 1940 in Liverpool.
★ At 15 he became interested in rock and roll.
★ 1963–64: Beatlemania breaks out in the UK and USA.
★ Beatles formed in 1960 with Paul McCartney, George Harrison and Stuart Sutcliffe (who died in 1962).
★ Failed his exams in 1957.
★ When he left school John enrolled at the Liverpool College of Art.
★ Invitation to play in Hamburg, Germany was the first big break for the group.
★ Beatles played regularly in a Liverpool club, the Cavern.
★ Brian Epstein, a record-shop owner, became their manager and steered the group to success.

Looking at the issues

For group discussion:

Ideas for writing

> A celebrity is a person who works hard all his life to become known, then wears dark glasses to avoid being recognised.
>
> *Fred Allen*

★ What do *you* think are the advantages and disadvantages of being famous?

Chapter 7

The Other Olympics

The modern Olympic Games were first held in Athens in 1896, and the first Winter Olympics followed in 1924. However, in 1960 a new dimension was added with the first Paralympic Games, and the Special Olympics began in 1968.

Extract

1 The Paralympics for people with physical disabilities and the Special Olympics for people with learning disabilities 5 (mental handicap) enable thousands of athletes to show the world the true meaning of the Olympic spirit.

The idea of sport for 10 disabled people came from Dr Ludwig Guttman, who used it in the treatment of paraplegics (people paralysed as a result of injuries to the spinal cord) in the Second World War. After the 15 war, he pioneered competitive sport for the paralysed. On the day the 1948 Olympic Games were opened in London, sixteen ex-service men and women took part in an archery contest at Stoke Mandeville, the famous hospital near London where paralysed victims of the war were treated.

20 From this small beginning grew the annual International Stoke Mandeville Games, a worldwide sports movement, and a special stadium was built at Stoke Mandeville in 1969. Every fourth year since 1960, the Games have been held if possible in the country hosting the Olympics. These 'parallel' games, called the

25 Paralympics, are now staged immediately after the Olympics, and in 1996 some of the events gained full Olympic status, with the winners receiving Olympic medals.

Never was the Olympic motto 'The important thing is not winning, but taking part ...' so appropriate as at the Special

30 Olympics. The Games, for people with learning disabilities, began in 1968 at Soldier Field, in Chicago, USA. They were set up largely through the efforts of people such as Eunice Kennedy Shriver, a sister of President John F. Kennedy, and the 1960 Olympic decathlon gold-medallist, Rafer Johnson. Summer and winter

35 international Games are now held every four years.

The aim of Special Olympics is to help people with learning disabilities to 'discover their full human potential and to bring them into the mainstream of life and work through sports training and competition.' Today, Special Olympics is the largest

40 amateur sports organisation in the world, with programmes operating in some 120 countries, and nearly a million athletes taking part. Coaches learn how to break down each sports skill into tasks which can be learned one by one.

An entry of 6,500 athletes for the 1995 Summer games means

45 2,000 coaches, 15,000 family members and 45,000 volunteers also participating. All athletes who enter a Special Olympics competition receive an award. In Special Olympics, nobody is a failure. They are all successes.

Taking a closer look ...

1 Explain in your own words the basic difference between the Paralympics and the Special Olympics as outlined in the first paragraph (lines 1–8). *(2 marks)*

2 Read paragraph two (lines 9–19).
   a) Explain when and why the idea of sport for disabled people came about. *(2 marks)*

   b) Write down the word from paragraph two which shows Dr
       Guttman was the first to introduce the idea of sport
       competitions for disabled people.   *(1 mark)*

3 Are the Paralympics always held in the same country as the main
   Games? Quote an expression from paragraph three (lines 20–27) in
   support of your answer.   *(1 mark)*

4 In your own words, explain why 1996 was a landmark in the
   history of the Paralympic Games.   *(2 marks)*

5 Explain how the name 'Paralympics' has been formed.   *(2 marks)*

6 Read the opening sentence of paragraph four (lines 28–30).
   a) What main difference is suggested between the aims of
       the competitors in the Paralympics and the Special Olympics?
                                                     (2 marks)
   b) Explain how the word order in this sentence helps express its
       meaning effectively.   *(2 marks)*

7 Read paragraph five (lines 36–43).
   In your own words, explain the two aims of the Special Olympics.
                                                     (2 marks)

8 In paragraphs five and six (lines 36–48), a large number of statistics
   are given. Referring to at least one example, explain clearly the
   effect of this.   *(2 marks)*

9 'In Special Olympics, nobody is a failure. They are all successes'
   (lines 47–48). Explain clearly what the author means by this.
                                                     (2 marks)

TOTAL MARKS: 20

Focus on language

Parenthesis

Parenthesis is the name given to a word, or words, inserted into a
sentence to comment or to give more information. The plural is
parentheses.

A parenthesis can be omitted from a sentence without affecting
the basic grammatical structure and sense of the sentence. For
example,

> The Olympic Games – which originated in Greece – were
> held in Athens in 1896.

This sentence would still make sense if the parenthesis within the dashes – which gives additional information – were to be omitted.

A parenthesis must always be enclosed in a **pair** of punctuation marks to separate it from the rest of the sentence: commas, dashes or round brackets may be used. Brackets are generally viewed as giving the *strongest* separation from the sentence, then dashes, with commas giving the *least* sense of separation.

If the parenthesis comes at the end of the sentence, and it is introduced by a comma or dash, a full stop only is required at the end of the sentence. If a round bracket is used to open the parenthesis, a closing round bracket is required as well as a full stop.

For practice (1)

In line 5, the writer of the extract uses brackets to provide an **explanation** or **alternative expression** for 'learning disabilities' – 'mental handicap'.

★ Can you explain why the writer uses brackets in paragraph two (lines 13–14)?
★ Find TWO examples from paragraph three (lines 20–27) of a parenthesis enclosed by a pair of *commas*.

For practice (2)

Punctuate the parentheses in the following sentences using brackets, dashes or commas as seems appropriate.

1 Dr Ludwig Guttman a famous German doctor used sport as a method of treatment.

2   Rafer Johnson won a gold medal for the decathlon at the Rome Olympics 1960.

3   In 1948 on the same day the Olympics opened in London the first competition for paraplegics was held at Stoke Mandeville.

4   The Olympic Games for the physically disabled Paralympics are also held every four years.

5   John F Kennedy US President from 1961 to 1963 was the famous brother of Eunice Kennedy Shriver.

Looking at the issues

In the first Games for the disabled at Stoke Mandeville, the chosen sport was archery. Why do you think that was a particularly suitable choice?

Make notes on the following topics. Then discuss them in groups.

★ 'In 1996, some of the events gained full Olympic status, with the winners receiving Olympic medals' (lines 26–27). Do you think that disabled athletes should receive exactly the same recognition as able-bodied ones? What arguments might be made for and against this? Why do you think only some of the events gained full Olympic status?

★ Discuss the nature of various Olympic events. Can you think of any in which disabled competitors might compete on equal terms or almost equal terms?

★ Within the Paralympics and Special Olympics themselves, competitors have a range of disabilities. How far is it possible to make these events fair to all the competitors? How much does this matter?

Ideas for writing

★ From your own knowledge and observation, write an essay discussing how well you feel the needs of the physically disabled, such as wheelchair users, are catered for in this country.

★ Recently there has been a move to integrate children with special needs (for example, blind or deaf children, or those with learning difficulties) into mainstream education rather than accommodate them in separate schools tailored to their requirements. Write a discursive essay for or against this, considering the advantages and disadvantages both to the children themselves and to the children already in mainstream education.

Chapter 8

Secrets of the Picts

On a promontory on Scotland's Moray coast is the village of Burghead. It lies on the site of a huge prehistoric fortress constructed by the Picts, a people who lived in Scotland in ancient times. Within the boundaries of the fortress is the mysterious Burghead well.

Extract

1   The present village of Burghead was built between 1805 and 1809 and, unfortunately for the archaeologist, its construction obliterated half of the largest Pictish fort known. However, several old maps recorded the plan of the original fort. Natural
5   terracing at the end of the promontory was adapted to create an upper and lower enclosure within the fort, outlined by ramparts, and at least three ramparts and ditches were dug across the neck of the promontory, enclosing an area of almost 3 hectares. These outer defences were probably built of earth
10   and rubble, but the inner fort was enclosed by massive walls. It was this handy source of stone that was used to build the harbour of the modern village, and there are tantalising records ➤

of the carved slabs that were found – and then built into the quay.

15   We are told of 'mouldings and carved figures, particularly of a bull', and it is tempting to imagine the great wall in its heyday, embellished with carvings, and prominent among them that symbol of strength and power: the bull. Thirty bull-stones are mentioned in old records, and more may have passed unnoticed,

20   but six have since been re-discovered during repairs and alterations to the harbour. The bulls are virtually identical, about 400mm long, and each is a masterpiece of carving, with glaring eyes and lowered head, muscular limbs and solid hooves – and in two cases an angrily swishing tail. The scale of the fort and the

25   bull-carvings imply an importance within the Pictish kingdom that is in keeping with the grandeur of the Burghead Well.

The well is an astounding structure. A flight of twenty rock-cut steps leads down towards what appears to be a huge black hole in the grassy slope – it could be the setting for Orpheus daring to

30   enter the underworld. Once your eyes adjust to the gloom at the bottom of the steps, you find yourself at the threshold of a large square chamber cut into solid bedrock, with a platform surrounding the central tank and a basin and pedestal in opposite corners. The well looks bottomless through the dark water but in

35   fact the tank is only 1.3 metres deep.

It is difficult to tell the original work from later modifications, but it seems likely that this was always a well of imposing proportions, suited to the needs of a large community, whatever those needs may have been aside from a domestic water supply.

40   Given the importance of water gods to their Celtic ancestors, the pagan Picts may also have had water rituals. The traditional method of execution among the Picts was drowning, even for important political prisoners of royal blood; two such executions are recorded in the 730s, one of the victims the 'King of Atholl',

45   the ruler of a frontier area between the Picts and the Scots. The curious scene depicted on the cross slab at Glamis Manse in Angus may illustrate such an execution, in which the victims ➤

Extract continued

were plunged head first into a great cauldron. It seems possible
that the Burghead Well may have had a similar purpose.

50   It may not be entirely coincidence that Burghead should be
the scene for a re-emergence in later times of a fire-festival: the
Clavie, a barrel of tar on a pole, is carried burning round the
village in January and brought to rest on a plinth that caps a well-
preserved remnant of one of the old Pictish ramparts. This
55   unusual survival of a tradition rooted in pagan times may reflect,
however faintly, the powerful role once played by the great
Pictish fort.

Taking a closer look ...

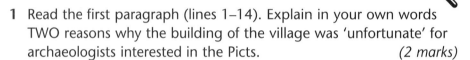

1   Read the first paragraph (lines 1–14). Explain in your own words
    TWO reasons why the building of the village was 'unfortunate' for
    archaeologists interested in the Picts.   *(2 marks)*

2   Explain in your own words how the Picts used the natural shape of
    the land to create a fort.

                                                         (2 marks)

3   Explain exactly what the author means when she says the old
    records of carved slabs are 'tantalising' (line 12).   *(2 marks)*

4   Read lines 15–24.
    a)   In your own words, explain TWO pieces of evidence which
         reveal the bull-carvings were of great importance to the Picts.
                                                         (2 marks)
    b)   Suggest and explain ONE reason why the bull was such a
         popular image with the Picts.   *(2 marks)*

5   In the description of the well in the third paragraph (lines 27–35),
    the author creates a dramatic atmosphere. Select any TWO phrases
    and explain how each of them contributes to this effect. Give a
    separate explanation for each of your chosen phrases.   *(4 marks)*

6   Read lines 37–49. The author suggests more than one purpose for
    the well. What does he suggest was the *main* purpose of the well?
    Explain your answer.   *(2 marks)*

7 Read lines 40–49.

    a) In your own words, explain TWO pieces of evidence the author has for suggesting that the well was used for executions.

(2 marks)

    b) Do you think the author is entirely convinced of his own theory about the executions? QUOTE a word or expression to support your answer. *(1 mark)*

8 Read the account of the present-day fire-festival in lines 50–54. Suggest ONE reason why the present day inhabitants of the village of Burghead carry out this strange custom. *(1 mark)*

TOTAL MARKS: 20

Focus on language

Dictionary work

For practice (1)

Each of the following words is taken from the story 'Secrets of the Picts'. Pick the meaning you think most closely matches its use in the passage:

obliterated (line 3)   a) blotted out b) covered c) damaged d) replaced

promontory (line 5)   a) rock b) headland c) hill d) beach

embellished (line 17)   a) covered up b) decorated c) topped d) supported

virtually (line 21)   a) almost b) truly c) surprisingly d) totally

pagan (line 41)   a) olden b) prehistoric c) past d) heathen

One of the options is a dictionary definition of the word. Check your answers with a dictionary.

For practice (2)

Find the twelve words in the passage for which the following are the dictionary definitions. The paragraph where each word is to be found is given to help you.

Definition	Word

paragraph one (lines 1–14)
  1 mounds or walls for defence
  2 landing stage for loading ships	

paragraph two (lines 15–26)
  3 time of most success
  4 noticeable/conspicuous
  5 suggest	

paragraph three (lines 27–35):
  6 amazing
  7 doorway/entrance	

paragraph four (lines 36–49)
  8 ceremonies
  9 large metal pot for boiling
     liquids	

paragraph five (lines 50–57) 10 accident/chance 11 reappearance 12 square block serving as a base	
Total marks: 12	

Looking at the issues

Make notes on the following topics. Then discuss them in groups.

★ Why do you think some people believe it is important to keep in touch with our past, even a distant past like the time of the Picts? The builders of the new village at Burghead did not think it important, and they put the old Pictish carved stones to a practical use in building the harbour. Discuss your own views on this.

★ The six bull-carvings mentioned in the passage are all on display to the public. Two are in the public library on Grant Street in the village of Burghead itself; two are in the museum at the nearby town of Elgin; one is in the Museum of Scotland in Edinburgh; and one is in the British Museum in London. If you were to visit the fort at Burghead for yourself, you would not have to go far to see one of the famous carvings. Discuss whether it is better to keep interesting finds near to the place they were found, or whether they should be moved to a large museum in a centre such as Edinburgh or London, where more people would have a chance to see them.

Ideas for writing

★ Imagine you are a guide and have been asked to show a school party around the fortress. Write a short script you would use to capture the pupils' interest.

★ Write a short story based on one of the ancient 'water rituals' using the Burghead well as a setting.

★ Imagine you are present at the modern fire-festival of the clavie at Burghead. Write a description of the event as vividly as you can.

★ Write a reflective essay on the subject of studying the past, exploring all the ways in which we can benefit from it.

Chapter 9

£89 Million Boost for Scotland

This report comes from *Pik-Up,* the in-house magazine of Glasgow Prestwick Airport.

Extract

1 No-frills flights from Glasgow Prestwick Airport have had a sky-high impact
5 on the Scottish economy, according to recent independent research.

Visitors flying
10 into Glasgow Prestwick International Airport with Ryanair alone pumped up to £89 million into Scotland – and new flights by the carrier are expected to make this figure grow even more. Inbound passengers spent 2.4 million nights in Scotland in the twelve month period,
15 staying eight nights on average. Ryanair carried almost as many visitors as outbound Scots.

The findings were revealed by economic development consultants SQW and survey experts NFO World Group in an interim report for Scottish Enterprise Ayrshire.

20 Researchers calculated that Ryanair's Prestwick flights support 1500–2000 Scottish jobs, with major economic benefits from Greater Glasgow to the Highlands and Islands. They reckoned the average spend in Scotland to be £215 a trip.

Around 90% of the 831 passengers interviewed said that the
25 fare was an 'important' or 'very important' reason for their trip.

Extract continued

Around 42% were holidaying; 38% visiting friends and relatives; and only 14% travelling on business. Since the start of the survey, Ryanair has doubled its Prestwick routes, now expecting an average daily passenger tally of around 8000 for the year ending
30 31 March 2004.

Michael Cawley, Ryanair's deputy chief executive, said: 'The survey is entirely consistent with Ryanair's beliefs – that Ryanair services generate inbound travel that would not have happened without the routes; that Ryanair generates additional short breaks
35 in addition to main holidays; that price is the main reason for travel, and that the internet is the most dominant booking source for flights.'

Scottish Enterprise Ayrshire chief executive Evelyn McCann welcomed the findings and was particularly cheered at the
40 estimated £18 million Ryanair was reckoned to bring into Ayrshire alone.

She comments: 'Having a high-profile operator like Ryanair based at Prestwick also contributes to the reputation and credibility of Ayrshire as a business location.' She added: 'The
45 research shows that inbound passenger awareness of Ayrshire itself is increasing since the introduction of these routes.'

Taking a closer look ...

1 Which of the following describes the purpose of this article best?
   a) to help advertise the flights operated by Ryanair
   b) to show the advantages that Prestwick Airport brings to Scotland
   c) both a) and b)
   d) neither a) nor b)   *(1 mark)*

2 Explain what is meant by the following phrases:
   a) no-frills flights (line 1)
   b) independent research (lines 7–8)
   c) inbound passengers (line 13)   *(6 marks)*

3 a) What does the expression 'sky-high impact' (line 4) mean?
   b) What makes it a particularly suitable expression?   *(2 marks)*

4 The writer uses various statistics to stress the economic advantages that Prestwick Airport brings to Scotland. QUOTE THREE examples.
   (3 marks)

5 In paragraph five (lines 24–30), the use of the word 'around' as in 'around 90% of the 831 passengers' shows that the figures are not exact. From elsewhere in the passage, QUOTE another word or phrase used for the same purpose.   *(1 mark)*

6 Explain why the writer uses a dash in line 32.   *(2 marks)*

7 Read paragraph seven (lines 38–41). QUOTE TWO words or phrases that show the reaction of Scottish Enterprise Chief Executive Evelyn McCann to the success of Ryanair and Prestwick Airport.   *(2 marks)*

8 Say whether each of these statements is true or false:
   a) Most passengers choose Ryanair because of the low fares.
   b) Between March 2003 and March 2004 Ryanair carried a total of 8,000 passengers.
   c) Most people who fly Ryanair do so for business purposes.
   (3 marks)

TOTAL MARKS: 20

Focus on Language

Formal writing

The passage in Chapter Three ('The *Real* James Bond') was written in an informal style. This one, however, uses mainly formal language. Here are some of the features of formal English writing.

The use of topic sentences
A topic sentence is a sentence which introduces the subject developed in more detail in the rest of the paragraph or the rest of the passage.

The opening sentence of the passage states:

> No-frills flights from Glasgow Prestwick Airport have had a sky-high impact on the Scottish economy, according to recent independent research.

This sentence is a topic sentence, as it mentions all the points that the rest of the passage discusses in more detail later on.

Facts rather than feelings

Formal writing deals more with facts and information than the writer's personal feelings or opinions.

Points are backed up with evidence

In this passage, the evidence is based on the results of research, presented in the form of statistics, and on quotations from experts.

FIND a piece of evidence from the passage to prove each of the following points:

Point	Evidence
Visitors who come to Scotland spend money when they get there.	
Most passengers think about the cost before booking a flight.	
Ryanair flights help to bring money into the area near Prestwick Airport.	

Word choice is different

A piece of formal writing is likely to use a wider and perhaps more difficult range of vocabulary.

The writing will be less personal and there will not be as many shortened forms like 'wouldn't', 'can't', etc.

For example, the following words, all of which are taken from the passage, could be described as formal. They are not often used in everyday conversations.

> generate   dominant   consultant
> high-profile   interim   credibility

Match these words with their correct definitions:

> the quality of being taken seriously, or believed in
> main, most important
> an expert who gives advice
> something done in the meantime; not the final thing
> to produce or create
> something that draws public attention

Ideas for writing

★ Look at a newspaper or magazine and cut out two articles, one of them being informal and the other formal.

★ Write a comparison of the two, commenting on such things as:

➤ choice of words
➤ use of abbreviations
➤ use of facts and figures
➤ whether opinions are expressed
➤ use of topic sentences
➤ print size, layout, etc.
➤ any other features.

Chapter 10

Cutting Spam out of your Mobile Diet

BBC News Online's Emma Clark looks at how text messages are being used as marketing tools.

Extract

1   If you did not get a Valentine's card from your true love this year, perhaps you got a spam Valentine's message instead.

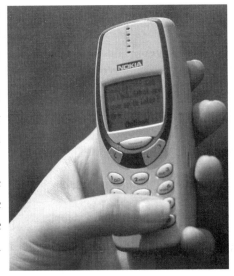

5   Spamming, or unsolicited messages sent by text to your mobile phone or email, is becoming ever more prevalent.

    One text message doing the
10   rounds this week is: 'If you were a chicken, you'd be impeccable ... Get loved up at lastminute. com/valentines'.

    You may or may not have read it – many people just press
15   delete before they are even halfway through the message.

    Others are simply bemused as to how the sender of the spam managed to acquire their mobile phone number, or email address (in this case, Lastminute says your contact details have been posted by someone who knows you and it promises not to reuse
20   them).

Hot marketing

These unsolicited messages are undoubtedly irritating and can also be costly if email is being downloaded at home or the recipient is duped into calling a premium-rate telephone
25   line.

➢

Extract continued

Despite this, however, text messaging has become the hottest new way to market a company, brand or product.

But if most of us tend to ditch the messages sight unseen, how are they effective?

30 Lars Becker, chief executive of SMS marketing company Flytxt, argues that text messaging campaigns can have a very high success rate if they are carefully designed.

A recent survey by the technology research firm, Forrester, also found that 56% of the responding companies planned to use text
35 messaging as a marketing tool in the future.

Flytxt itself has found that a well-crafted text message can get a response rate as high as 10% – for a relatively low cost.

Text campaigns

The company, which has devised text message campaigns for
40 clients such as Cadbury and Emap, uses the medium in a variety of ways.

For example, it runs text clubs designed to build customer loyalty for Emap's *Smash Hits* magazine, sending text messages containing pop gossip to members and inviting them to
45 participate in competitions.

But one of Flytxt's most well-known campaigns was for the chocolate maker Cadbury last summer.

Customers learnt whether they had won a competition by sending a text message to a
50 number on the chocolate bar wrapper.

The campaign enabled Cadbury's to collect information about the times when customers
55 ate certain bars and which other bars they liked.

> ### Did you know . . . ?
>
> In 2001, 13 per cent of children of primary school age owned a mobile phone.
>
> By 2004, the number had increased to 25 per cent.

Not spam?

Mr Becker, however, is careful to differentiate his company's tactics from the more unscrupulous senders of spam.

Extract continued

60   He says that recipients of messages are always given the chance to opt out from receiving any further messages.

Flytxt also only uses customer information it collects itself – with permission – or from reputable databases.

'The danger is that the market follows the email model, which
65 has automatic associations with spam,' he explains. 'And it got a bad name.'

To this end, Flytxt helped found the Wireless Marketing Association, which has established a code of best practice for text marketers.

70 'We are against unsolicited messages and we want to protect the industry,' says Mr Becker.

Taking a closer look . . .

1 Explain how the writer has made the title of the passage effective.
(2 marks)

2 Which sentence between lines 1 and 15 would you say was the topic sentence of the whole passage? (Write out only the first three words.) *(1 marks)*

3 a) What do most people do as soon as they receive a text message of the kind described here? *(1 mark)*

   b) In your own words, explain why some people are 'bemused' (line 16) by these messages. *(2 marks)*

4 Read lines 22–25. In your own words, explain one of the ways these unwanted messages can be costly for the person receiving them.
(2 marks)

5 a) Which words in lines 26–30 indicate to the reader that the passage is moving on to discuss a different point?

   b) In your own words, explain what this point is. *(2 marks)*

6 Quote a statistic that shows that it is worthwhile for companies to use text messages as a way of advertising. *(1 mark)*

7 Read lines 39–56. Describe two examples of text advertising devised by Flytxt. *(4 marks)*

8 In lines 58–71, Lars Becker defends the methods used by his company. In your own words, explain one of the reasons he gives in his defence. *(2 marks)*

9 In earlier chapters, we looked at the differences between formal and informal language.
  a) Quote an example of formal language from anywhere in the passage.
  b) Quote an example of informal language from anywhere in the passage.
  c) Would you say that this passage is mainly formal or mainly informal? *(3 marks)*

TOTAL MARKS: 20

Focus on language (1)

Dictionary work

Each of the following words is used in the passage. Pick the meaning you think most closely matches its use in the passage.

unsolicited (line 5)   a) not asked for b) not welcome c) unexpected

duped (line 24)   a) persuaded b) forced c) tricked

devised (line 39)   a) invented b) written c) designed

unscrupulous (line 59)   a) careless b) dishonest c) unfair

tactics (line 59)   a) schemes b) methods c) tricks

reputable (line 63)   a) special b) well-known c) trustworthy

Focus on language (2)

Linking words

In Chapter Eleven, 'Citizens of the World', we will look at how a writer constructs an argument and uses linking words as pointers.

Twice in the passage above, the writer Emma Clark uses the word 'however' to make a point in opposition to the previous one.

For example:

> Mr Becker, <u>however</u>, is careful to differentiate his company's tactics from the more unscrupulous senders of spam.

This sentence moves the passage on from discussing the problems of spam to a discussion of how this particular company claims to send messages in a more acceptable way.

Linking words or phrases can be used to:

> ➤ **Make a point opposing the previous one**
> e.g. however, nevertheless, on the other hand
>
> ➤ **Add on a point supporting the previous one**
> e.g. moreover, furthermore, in addition, also, equally, in the same way
>
> ➤ **Draw a conclusion**
> e.g. therefore, thus, as a result, consequently, in conclusion

For practice

From the lists in the box above, choose the most suitable linking word or phrase to begin the second sentence in each of the following pairs.

(There will still be two separate sentences – you are not joining the two into one.)

1 The pitch was waterlogged. _____, the game had to be cancelled.

2 A mobile phone is very useful for keeping in touch with your friends. _____, it can be very valuable in emergencies.

3 My mother believes mobile phones are bad for your brain. _____, I couldn't live without mine!

4 The latest mobile phones are extremely light in weight. They can _____ take photographs.

5 I'd like to tell him exactly what I think of him. _____, it might be better not to say anything.

6 David didn't bother changing out of his wet clothes. _____, he caught a cold.

Looking at the issues

> WORRIES OVER HEALTH RISKS POSED BY MOBILE PHONES
>
> *(Newspaper headline)*

> **SCHOOL BANS USE OF MOBILE PHONES AMONG UNDER-16s**
>
> *(Newspaper headline)*

> *Figures issued by the Home Office suggest that, in 2001, 700,000 mobile phones were stolen.*

★ In groups, make a list of the advantages and the disadvantages of mobile phones.

★ Balance these up and reach a conclusion.

★ One member of the group should report his/her findings to the rest of the class.

Chapter 11

Citizens of the World

A society which is 'multi-ethnic' is one which is composed of people from many different cultures. Most of the developed countries of the world are now becoming 'multi-ethnic' as people from more deprived areas move there in order to escape from problems in their native lands. In the following extract, the writer looks at some of the questions raised by this migration.

Extract

1   As societies around the world continue to become increasingly multi-ethnic, the arguments about racism tend to be less about whether it is wrong or right. Instead, the most pressing problem is how to ensure that diverse communities live without racial
5   tension, in a society free of racial prejudice and discrimination. We are now going to look at some of the different opinions and arguments that have surfaced in the search for a multi-ethnic society in which everybody has equal opportunities in life.
    Today, there are 150 million people living outside their
10 countries of birth. At least 22 million have been forced to move from their homes because of war or racial persecution. We already

know that the multi-ethnic societies are built on a history of migration. We also know that the arrival of migrants into a society can create racial tension. Some people argue that this
15   tension is the result of a new kind of racism: that of discrimination and prejudice against people who want and need to improve their lives. But whether migration actually does create tension depends on the actions of governments across the world.

Since most of the migrant populations are from less developed
20   countries, some people argue that they bring unskilled and uneducated individuals into society. If migrants have less 'economic value', there might be more strain on public services like health, housing and education. In the USA, for example, economists argue that if the government supports healthcare for Hispanic[1] migrants,
25   then others in society will have to pay more for health insurance. There is also a concern that migrants will become 'second-class' citizens, and that ghetto[2]-like communities will grow. This division could mean that certain communities are excluded and less likely to become involved in the rest of society. To avoid this, some people
30   think that governments should manage migration by limiting the number of people allowed into a country. They think that governments should only select those individuals who fit the needs of a society – for example, those with skills, like doctors or computer experts, who can immediately contribute to the economy.

35   However, some people argue that managed migration makes matters worse. If only skilled migrants are encouraged, then there will be fewer skilled people in less developed countries where the skills are needed most. This could lead to more poverty and even more people wanting to leave. The United Nations also estimates
40   that, by the year 2025, 159 million migrant workers will be needed to keep the European economy growing. This is because birth rates in Europe are falling and there is a need for both skilled and unskilled workers. To keep the European economy growing, and to offer improved lifestyles for those in less developed countries,
45   some argue that it is more sensible to relax migration controls and allow people to move more freely as citizens of the world. ❑

[1] From Spanish-speaking countries, especially those in Central and South America.
[2] An area of a city, usually poor and densely populated, where a minority group lives apart.

Taking a closer look ...

1 a) Read the first paragraph (lines 1–8). Is the ethnic mix in societies becoming more, becoming less, or staying about the same?

   b) QUOTE an expression from the first sentence in support of your answer. *(2 marks)*

2 In lines 1–3, the writer states that people are no longer discussing whether racism is right or wrong. In your own words, explain what the writer says the 'most pressing problem' is now. *(2 marks)*

3 At the end of paragraph one, the writer states that he thinks the aim should be for a society 'in which everybody has equal opportunities in life' (line 8). From your own knowledge, suggest ONE example of the 'equal opportunities' the writer might have in mind. *(1 mark)*

4 a) In paragraph two, we are told that only 22 million of the 150 million people who have left their homes did so because of wars or persecution. Can you suggest why the others have moved to the developed countries? *(1 mark)*

   b) QUOTE an expression from this paragraph (lines 9–18) which sums up the reason given by the writer for the majority of migrants moving to a new country. *(1 mark)*

5 According to the writer, what is the main factor responsible for whether or not the arrival of migrants will create tension in the community? *(1 mark)*

6 In paragraph three (lines 19–34), the writer presents one set of views.

   a) In your own words, sum up the problems concerning migrants, according to 'some people'. *(4 marks)*

   b) Explain in your own words the suggested solution described in lines 29–34. *(2 marks)*

7 Why do you think the words 'economic value' (lines 21–22) are in inverted commas? *(2 marks)*

8 Read lines 35–45. In your own words, explain why some people think admitting only skilled migrants will make the situation worse. *(2 marks)*

9 What further reason is given in the last paragraph for encouraging more migrants into Europe? *(2 marks)*

TOTAL MARKS: 20

Focus on language

Discursive writing

The extract above is an example of **discursive writing**. Discursive writing presents *two* sides of an argument.

In the case of this piece, the **structure** of the argument falls into four sections:

Paragraph 1: introduction of the topic to be discussed (migration); a statement of what the writer will do (look at different opinions and arguments on the topic of migration)

Paragraph 2: facts and statistics about the topic (migration)

Paragraph 3: opinions and arguments in favour (of restrictions on migration)

Paragraph 4: opinions and arguments against (restrictions on migration)

This basic plan can be followed for a piece of discursive writing on any topic that has two opposing arguments. You would usually want to add a fifth paragraph, in which you **evaluate** the two sides of the argument (rate how good or bad they are) and present a **conclusion** (a summing-up).

It will be important to use suitable **linking words or phrases** in order to show how the arguments relate to each other. Words like 'also' and 'moreover' build on one side of an argument, while expressions like 'however' and 'on the other hand' indicate a contrast. (See Chapter Ten for more examples of linking words.)

The author of the piece of writing on migration has presented his arguments clearly. The following task will help to reveal the techniques he has used.

For practice

1 Which sentence in paragraph one clearly sets out what the writer intends to do? Write down the first and last words of the sentence.

2 In paragraph two (lines 9–18), the author presents facts. For example, 'There are 150 million people living outside their countries of birth.' Pick out TWO more statements from this paragraph that show the writer is presenting *facts* rather than introducing *opinions* at this stage.

3   In paragraphs three and four (lines 19–46), the author presents opinions rather than facts. He makes this clear by using expressions such as 'some people argue' (line 35). From paragraphs three and four, pick out THREE more expressions which clearly show he is presenting *opinion* rather than fact.

4   The author shows that these opinions may or may not be valid by using expressions which reveal there is room for doubt: e.g., 'there might be more strain...'
Find ONE more expression from lines 35–46 which shows he believes the opinions may not be valid.

5   Throughout the article, the author frequently uses linking words to build up his arguments on each side. For example, 'There is also a concern' (line 26). Suggest another word or phrase he could have used instead of 'also'.

6   a) Which expression is used in paragraph four (lines 35–46) to show that the other side of the argument will follow?

    b) Suggest one other word or phrase with a similar meaning that the author could have used instead.

Looking at the issues

Make notes on the following topics. Then discuss them in groups.

★ Read again the arguments for and against 'managed migration' in paragraphs three and four of the text. Which arguments do you find most convincing? Are there any flaws in any of the arguments? Can you think of other problems which may arise through following the suggested policies? Prepare a conclusion to the discussion in the form of a fifth paragraph.

★ In the text, the author raises the topic of the conflict which may arise within a multiracial society. From your own knowledge, make a list of the causes of this type of conflict. Rank the items on your list in order of seriousness. Then suggest possible solutions which might help to promote the ideal of a multi-ethnic society free of racial tension.

Topics for writing

Write a short piece of discursive writing on *one* of the following topics using the basic plan given above. You may argue for one side only, or present a balanced argument. You might need to use reference books or the internet to find out the necessary facts for the second stage of your argument. You should add a fifth paragraph summing up the arguments and offering a conclusion.

★ The voting age in this country should be reduced to 16.
★ Animals should/should not be used in the testing of new drugs.
★ Fee paying schools should/should not be available as an alternative to state schools for those who can afford them.
★ Women are just as acceptable as men in all professions.

Chapter 12

The Greatest Runner of All Time?

At each Olympiad, old records are broken and new ones set. However, the achievements of Czech athlete Emil Zatopek at the Helsinki Olympics in 1952 have never been equalled.

Extract

1　Some Olympic champions do not just win, they win in style. The star of the 1952 Games in Helsinki was no such stylist.

5　According to one watcher, he ran 'like a man who had just been stabbed in the heart.' It was also said about him that 'he does everything wrong except

10　win.' But no one could deny this awkward-looking runner's brilliance. Emil Zatopek was an all-time great.

　　Czech army officer Zatopek arrived in Helsinki in 1952 as the

15　reigning Olympic champion at 10,000 metres. In 1948 he had also won a silver medal in the 5000 metres. But now he was 30 years old, and he had not been on top form before the Games. Nevertheless, he planned to compete in a *third* event within eight days in Helsinki: the marathon. He had never run a marathon

20　before, but he believed his tough training methods would stand him in good stead.

　　His first event was the 10,000 metres. The rest of the field was strong, but no one else could live with Zatopek's blistering pace. He won by about 100 metres. Next up was the 5000 metres: heats

25　first, then the final – which turned out to be one of the most exciting Olympic races ever. Usually in the last lap, Zatopek simply burned off most of his challengers. This time, soon after he kicked for home, three runners stormed past *him*. This had never happened to him before.

30 With 250 metres to go, Herbert Schade of Germany, Britain's Chris Chataway and France's Alain Mimoun looked like sharing out the medals between them. Desperately Zatopek tried to catch up. With 180 metres to go, all four runners were in a line across the track. The head of the one on the outside was rolling in agony,

35 his arms were thrashing, his chest was heaving: Emil Zatopek – and 180 metres further on, he breasted the tape to win gold.

Later that afternoon, Zatopek heard that his wife, Dana, had just won a gold medal in the javelin. 'At present,' he joked with reporters, 'the score of the contest in the Zatopek family is 2–1.

40 This result is too close. To restore some prestige I will try to improve on the margin – in the marathon race.' He did it …

After 15 kilometres, he was in the lead alongside Britain's Jim Peters. Six weeks before, Peters had run the fastest marathon in history. Zatopek, of course, had never run a marathon in his life.

45 He turned to Peters and asked in perfect English: 'The pace, is it fast enough?' Peters had started too quickly, and now he felt exhausted. But he did not want Zatopek to know that, so he replied, 'No, it's too slow.' Zatopek thought about this, then raced ahead – to a stunning victory.

50 Zatopek's triple-gold haul in Helsinki was a magnificent achievement. No one has ever repeated it. But Zatopek was not just a brilliant runner and racer, he was a true Olympian too. In the 1960s another magnificent distance runner emerged: Ron Clarke of Australia. Everyone knew Clarke was the world's best

55 and he had the records to prove it. But although he gave his all at Tokyo in 1964 and at Mexico City in 1968 – and helped to make both Games so memorable – he came away without a single Olympic victory. On his way back to Australia in 1968, he stopped over in Europe to see his old friend Emil Zatopek. On

60 parting from him, Zatopek gave him a small gift, which Clarke opened only when he got home. Inside the wrapping was Zatopek's 10,000 metres gold medal from 1952.

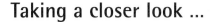

Taking a closer look ...

1 Explain what the expression 'all-time' adds to the meaning of the sentence, 'Emil Zatopek was an all-time great' (line 13).   *(1 mark)*

2 a) In paragraph one (lines 1–13) there are two quotations that describe Zatopek's running style. Select ONE of these, and in your own words explain what you think the speaker meant by it.   *(2 marks)*

   b) Find the descriptive phrase from paragraph one that sums up these comments.   *(1 mark)*

3 Read lines 14–21. What success had Zatopek had in the 1948 Olympic Games?   *(2 marks)*

4 In your own words, give TWO reasons why Zatopek might have been expected to do less well in the 1952 Games than in 1948.   *(2 marks)*

5 'He won by about 100 metres' (line 24). How does the author's sentence structure emphasise how easy this race was for Zatopek? *(1 mark)*

6 Explain the function of the colon and the dash in the sentence 'Next up ... races ever.' (lines 24–26).   *(2 marks)*

7 a) Explain clearly what the writer means by the expression 'burned off' (line 27) in the sentence 'Zatopek simply burned off most of his challengers.'   *(2 marks)*

   b) What figure of speech does the author use in the expression 'burned off'?   *(1 mark)*

8 'With 250 metres to go... With 180 metres to go ...' (lines 30–36). Explain exactly the effect you think the writer is aiming at by opening each of these sentences with a similar phrase.   *(2 marks)*

9 Look at the structure of the last sentence in paragraph four (lines 34–36). Instead of saying 'Zatopek's head ...', he says 'the head of the one on the outside...' Can you suggest a reason for this and for putting Zatopek's name *after* the description of the runner's pain?   *(2 marks)*

10 a) Read Zatopek's remarks to the reporters in lines 38–41. Explain what he meant by 'This result is too close.'   *(2 marks)*

   b) Name ONE quality this remark might seem to reveal about Zatopek's personality.   *(1 mark)*

11 Read lines 42–49. Give TWO reasons why Zatopek's victory in the marathon could not have been predicted. *(2 marks)*

12 Explain how the anecdote about Ron Clarke makes an effective ending to this article. *(2 marks)*

TOTAL MARKS: 25

Focus on language

Italics

'Italics' is the name given to a sloping style of type.

For practice (1)

Explain clearly the effect of the author's use of italics in the following sentences from the extract on Emil Zatopek:

1 'Nevertheless, he planned to compete in a *third* event within eight days in Helsinki: the marathon.' (lines 18–19)

2 'Usually in the last lap, Zatopek simply burned off most of his challengers. This time, soon after he kicked for home, three runners stormed past *him*.' (lines 26–29)

Italics have several uses.

a) They are used to mark titles. For example, *The Times* newspaper, *Great Expectations* by Charles Dickens. You will see this use in print, and you can use it yourself when writing on a computer or word processor.

b) They are used to show foreign words or phrases, as in 'In Japan, the *gaijin*, or foreigners, find it hard to be accepted.'

c) They are used to show that special emphasis is to be placed on certain words: 'Fire doors must not be locked at *any* time.'

d) They may indicate a particular tone, such as irony or suspense. For example, '*Very* nice company for other people's children!'

e) They are used where a variation in typefaces is wanted. For example, in most dictionaries, the pronunciation and derivations of words are usually in italics to separate them from the definition of the word.

f) Italics are frequently used for quotations, such as extracts of poetry.

g) Some authors use italics instead of inverted commas to indicate direct speech. A well-known example of this is the novel *Sunset Song,* by Lewis Grassic Gibbon.

For practice (2)

Consider why the italics have been used in each of the examples below. From the list above, choose the letter that best describes their use.

1   Jim did not leave his wife; she left *him.*

2   Long Rob looked down at the dead man. He said *He was a fine neighbour* and went out and closed the door.

3   At the head of the line of men rode the fat Belgian *commandante* on a black horse.

4   My sister likes to read *Smash Hits.*

5   My favourite lines of poetry are by Robert Frost:

> *Nature's first green is gold,*
> *The hardest hue to hold.*

6   **liver** *liver, n.* a fanciful bird on the arms of the city of Liverpool. [Formed from *Liverpool*]

7   As I looked back at the pyramid, the blood froze in my veins. *A thin column of smoke was emerging from the point.*

For practice (3)

A common use of italics is to suggest a particular **tone**, such as irony, surprise, amazement, tension or anger.

For example, In S E Hinton's novel *The Outsiders,* the teenage narrator, Ponyboy, describes an occasion when he and some members of his gang, the Greasers, attend a church service. The gang are sitting at the back of the church. A boy nicknamed Two-Bit starts misbehaving noisily with one of the others which makes the congregation look round in annoyance. Ponyboy continues, 'Then Two-Bit *waved* at them.'

Here the use of italics in 'waved' is very effective in suggesting the tone. It emphasises the outrageous cheekiness of the wave, and it also suggests the embarrassment of Ponyboy, who is telling the story.

Decide what the use of italics suggests about the tone in each of the following examples. You could do this by reading the example aloud to a partner.

1 I want the money *now*.

2 He is not at school as he was bitten by a *snake*?

3 We will *never* surrender.

4 Do you call her *beautiful*?

5 The towel was *filthy*.

6 Did *anyone* in this class pass Physics last year?

7 I learned that you can *always* run fast if you think there are fifty or a hundred men after you.

8 That is *my* seat.

Looking at the issues:

Make notes on the following topics. Then discuss them in groups.

★ 'Some Olympic champions do not just win, they win in style.' Think of different ways in which this statement might be true. In the light of the whole article, discuss whether or not you felt Zatopek could be said to have won 'in style'. How important is it to win 'in style'?

★ Think about the feelings of the 'losers', Jim Peters and Ron Clarke, in the above article. Discuss how you think they might have felt and why: a) at the time of the event; b) soon after the Games were over; c) twenty years later.

★ In the past, the Olympic Games were strictly for amateurs only. Athletes were not allowed to take money, and professional athletes were barred from taking part. In what ways do you think this might be a better or worse situation than today, when most Olympic athletes are paid?

Ideas for writing

★ The Olympic motto is a Latin phrase, '*Citius, Altius, Fortius*', which means 'Faster, higher, stronger'. However, the unofficial motto of the Games is that 'it is not the winning but the taking part' which matters. Write a discursive essay on whether taking part is more important than winning. You may argue on one side or the other, or take a balanced viewpoint. You may refer to some of the examples from the extract in your essay.

★ Write a description of the opening or closing ceremony of an Olympic Games, presenting the scene as vividly as you can. Try to make use of the senses in your description. You may write either from memory or from your imagination.

Emile Zatopek with the runner up Reginald De Corno after winning the 1952 marathon.

Chapter 13

The Left-Handed Way

Around one in ten people in Britain today is left-handed. The writer of the following article looks at left-handedness in different ages and cultures and also at some of the problems and prejudices associated with being a left-hander.

Extract

1　Sinister. Gauche. Awkward. Insults applied by almost every civilisation to one of the most victimised groups in history. For thousands of years, mankind has had an unfair prejudice against those whose brains are wired in such a way that when they reach

5　for a cup or a pen they choose the left hand over the right. According to Professor Chris McManus, who has written a book on it, there has been a huge rise in left-handedness in recent years – a fourfold increase in the past century.

　　Why are there so many more left-handers now? And can it

10　really be true that they are more gifted, inspired and prone to genius? After all, Julius Caesar, Michelangelo and Pele are among their number. To answer the first question, you have to study the history of 'lefties', which is a not entirely happy one.

15 'Anthropologists have never found a single society where left-handedness is more valued than right-handedness,' says Prof McManus. 'There may have been practical reasons – for instance, when farm workers are scything a field, someone using their left hand would be more likely to injure their colleagues. Humans are always finding reasons to discriminate against people who are

20 different in any way.'

Discrimination is even built into language. 'Dextrous' – from the Latin for 'right' – means 'skilful' and 'coordinated'. However, the Latin word for left forms the root of the word *sinister*. The French-derived word *adroit* from *droit*, 'right', means 'clever',

25 whereas *gauche* ('left') means 'clumsy' and 'ill-mannered'.

The prejudice probably reached its peak in Victorian times. Then, left-handed children had their 'condition' beaten out of them. In fact, pure prejudice probably meant there were fewer left-handers born in the old days, says Prof McManus: 'Left-

30 handers would have been victimised and found it harder to find a partner, so would have had fewer children.'

The biological cause of left-handedness is unclear, but there is evidence that the range of talents is greater among the left-handed. Joan of Arc, Winston Churchill and Alexander the Great were left-handers, as were Paul McCartney and Jimi Hendrix, who

35 both learned to play the 'right-handed' guitar upside down. Marilyn Monroe was, and Nicole Kidman is, left-handed. The identity of Jack the Ripper may still be unknown but what we do know, from the way he used his knives, was that he was left-

40 handed.

Certainly, society is not geared for the left-handed. Simply writing from left to right puts southpaws at a disadvantage – in dragging the pen over the page they risk smudging the ink, and the writing position is awkward. Just about every piece of

45 technology – from scissors, to computer keyboards and mice – is geared for people who are right-handed. Left-handed soldiers are

at a particular disadvantage – automatic weapons discharge spent, red-hot cartridges to the right, into the face of the left-handed firer.

50   Whatever its cause, it is clear that like eye colour, height and the ability to run a four-minute mile, left-handedness is part of the natural variability in human beings.

Taking a closer look . . .

1 Read lines 1–2 'Sinister...history.' How does the author use sentence structure in these lines to make the opening of the article attract your attention?   *(2 marks)*

2 'Mankind has had an unfair prejudice against ...' (line 3)
Find another expression from the same paragraph which has a similar meaning to 'had an unfair prejudice against.'   *(1 mark)*

3 Read paragraph two (lines 9–13).
In your own words, briefly explain the two questions which the writer seeks to answer in the rest of the article.   *(2 marks)*

4 In lines 14–20, Professor McManus suggests two basic reasons for prejudice against left-handers.
  a) Without using the example of farm workers scything, explain what the writer means by 'practical reasons' in line 16. *(2 marks)*
  b) Explain the second reason in your own words.   *(2 marks)*

5 The writer claims languages reflect discrimination against the left-handed. Look at the evidence in lines 21–25. Explain clearly how far you find it convincing.   *(2 marks)*

6 Explain in your own words Professor McManus's theory in lines 28–31 as to why fewer left-handed people were being born.
                                                                    (2 marks)

7 Look at the list of celebrities in lines 34–38. Explain how convincing you find the list as proof for his view that 'the range of talents is greater among the left-handed'.   *(2 marks)*

8 In your own words, summarise the problems for left-handers as described in lines 41–49.   *(3 marks)*

9 Find words in the text that have the following definitions:
a) people who study human society and customs; b) to treat someone differently, usually unfavourably, because they are different.   *(2 marks)*

TOTAL MARKS: 20

Focus on language (1)

Dashes and hyphens

Dashes and hyphens are both small strokes, with the dash being wider than a hyphen. It is important to remember they are different, as they are used differently.

The **hyphen** (-) has two main uses. It is used to join two or more words to form a 'compound' word; for example, 'left-handed', 'red-hot'. It is also used to indicate that a word has been split at the end of a line of print if there is not enough room to put in the whole word.

The **dash** (–) is a punctuation mark which has several uses. These can be seen in the extract you have just read. It can be used like a colon as an *introducing* mark: to introduce an example, an explanation, a list or a summing-up of the statement before it. For example:

> There has been a huge rise in left-handedness in recent years – a fourfold increase in the past century. (lines 7–8)

Choosing a dash instead of a colon is a matter of personal preference, but the dash is generally considered to be more informal.

A pair of dashes can also be used – like a pair of brackets or a pair of commas –– to mark off a parenthesis (an extra piece of information) from the rest of the sentence. (For more information on parenthesis, see pages 39–40.) For example:

> 'Dextrous' – from the Latin word for 'right' – means 'skilful'.

★ Can you find ONE other example of *each* of these uses of the dash in the passage?
★ Can you find TWO other examples of expressions with hyphens in the passage?

For practice (1)

Add dashes and hyphens where required to the following sentences.

1 In sport superstition is common many tennisplayers bounce the tennisball a fixed number of times before serving.

2 Birds magpies in particular are the basis of many superstitions.

3 I am quite superstitious I never walk under a ladder or open an umbrella indoors.

4 The number thirteen is considered unlucky there were thirteen present at the Last Supper, for example.

5 The prejudice against lefthanded people persisted till modern times Japanese women could be divorced simply because they were lefthanded.

Focus on language (2)

Shades of meaning

'Discrimination is even built into language.' (line 21) This sentence from the extract means that a person's attitude to something may be revealed through word choice.

English is a language with a rich vocabulary. There are many words that appear to mean the same, but in fact may subtly suggest feelings of approval or disapproval.

Look at some of the words from the extract:

> Gifted   inspired   clever   skilful

These are words which might appear in a thesaurus as **synonyms**; words which mean approximately the same.

All of these words convey approval, but some do so more strongly than others. Can you rank these words in order, starting with the weakest and ending with the strongest in terms of approval?

For practice (2)

Look at the following lists of words. Rank them as you are asked. (You may find certain words equal in rank.)

1 *Rogue, rascal, criminal, law-breaker, villain.*
   Rank these in order of disapproval, with the least first.

2 *Neat, fussy, careful, tidy, meticulous, pernickety.*
   Rank these in order of approval, with the least first.

3 *Small, tiny, minute, miniature, little.*
Rank these in order of size, with the largest first.

Looking at the issues

★ Conduct a survey. Find out how many of your class are left-handed. Divide into groups, including one or more left-handed people in each group. Interview the left-handed people to find out what problems or difficulties they encounter and how they solve these. Are there any advantages to being left-handed?

★ Make notes on other irrational prejudices society may hold against individuals, e.g. those based on appearance. Then share your ideas with your group or class.

★ Make a study of superstitions. In groups, list various superstitions. Then consider whether they are likely to have a practical basis. Hold a survey among members of your group to find out which superstitions they themselves hold.

Ideas for writing

★ In the novel *To Kill a Mockingbird*, the plot involves a right-handed man being convicted of a crime which only a left-handed person could have done. Write a short story with a similar theme. You may choose to make the left-handed person innocent!

★ Choose one of the famous left-handed people mentioned in the extract. Use the internet or your nearest library to research his or her life. Then write a short biography of around 600 words. Alternatively, you could prepare your material in the form of a talk to the class.

★ Write a personal essay, describing and explaining your own superstitions and prejudices. You might also mention those held by people close to you, such as members of your family or friends.

Chapter 14

Pocahontas

Pocahontas was the American Indian princess who achieved fame as a peacemaker. She married a British settler but died on a trip to Britain at the age of 21. She is buried in the church at Gravesend in Kent, where there is also a statue of her.

Extract

1 Of the millions of Indians who have ever lived in North America, most people could probably name only three:
5 Hiawatha, the chief who organised the Iroquois into a Federation of Nations; Sitting Bull, who destroyed General Custer and his troops; and a
10 young girl called Pocahontas.

Pocahontas's story begins with the foundation of the British colony at Jamestown, Virginia, in 1607. This was a vulnerable settlement 60 miles (96
15 km) up river in mosquito-infested territory, surrounded by hostile Indians under their chief Powhatan. Within three months, 46 colonists, nearly half the total, had died of disease. The rest faced starvation as they were too weak to farm the land, and unfamiliar with the native fruits and berries that could save them. In
20 desperation, the ruling council turned to the strongest man among them, John Smith, and begged him to undertake the dangerous task of seeking help and supplies from the Indians.

Smith, an experienced mercenary soldier, travelled 50 miles (80 km) up the James River before being captured by Powhatan's

25 warriors. He might have been killed there and then, but he resourcefully played for time by showing the Indians his 'magic' compass with its needle moving apparently unaided. Eventually he was taken to Powhatan's camp, where the chief and his elders debated his fate. The sentence was death.

30 Smith was stretched out on the ground, where he was to be clubbed to death. But just as the first blow was about to be struck, the chief's 12-year-old daughter, Pocahontas, rushed forward and flung herself protectively across Smith's body, begging for his life. Smith was freed, adopted by the tribe, given Indian names and

35 returned to Jamestown with provisions.

Jamestown soon needed saving again. Although some 900 settlers had made the voyage in the first two years, there were only 100 left by 1610. However, in 1612 John Rolfe introduced tobacco and founded the basis of further prosperity. Two years

40 later, with the agreement of her father, Rolfe married Pocahontas and in 1616 he took her to England. There she was given celebrity status as 'Lady Rebecca, alias Pocahontas, who was taught by John Rolfe, her husband, and his friends, to speak English and learn English customs and manners.' The marriage brought about a

45 peace treaty with the Indians and heralded a period of growth and stability for the Jamestown settlement. Once again, Pocahontas had played her part in saving the colony.

But, at the age of 21, just as her husband was about to return to Jamestown with her, she contracted smallpox and died. Six

50 years later, the first of a series of devastating wars between Indians and settlers broke out. These were to destroy the Powhatan Indians and establish the military supremacy of the English in Virginia.

Taking a closer look ...

1 Read paragraph one (lines 1–10).
   a) In your own words, explain what the information about Hiawatha and Sitting Bull reveals about the history of American Indians and their relationship with the settlers from Europe.
   (2 marks)
   b) From the information given in paragraph one, explain ONE way in which Pocahontas seems to be different from the other famous Indians, Hiawatha and Sitting Bull. *(1 mark)*

2 a) Explain the meaning of 'vulnerable' (line 14).
   b) Show how the rest of the sentence makes the meaning of 'vulnerable' clear. *(2 marks)*

3 Read paragraph two (lines 11–22). In your own words, explain TWO reasons why the inhabitants of Jamestown were starving.
   (2 marks)

4 Suggest TWO reasons why John Smith was selected to approach the Indians. *(2 marks)*

5 a) Explain clearly the meaning of 'resourcefully' (line 26).
   (1 mark)
   b) Show how the rest of the sentence makes the meaning clear.
   (2 marks)

6 a) Consider Pocahontas's actions in lines 30–33. Explain TWO personal qualities of character which her actions reveal that she possessed. *(2 marks)*
   b) Suggest ONE reason why the tribe gave in to Pocahontas's pleas for mercy. *(1 mark)*

7 Read lines 34–35.
   a) Explain why it was surprising that the tribe treated John Smith so well after his life had been spared. *(2 marks)*
   b) Can you suggest a reason why they treated him as well as they did in the end? *(1 mark)*

8 Read lines 36–47. Referring closely to the text, but using your own words, explain the important contribution made by John Rolfe to the community at Jamestown. *(3 marks)*

9 Explain TWO pieces of evidence which show that John Rolfe's marriage to Pocahontas was based on love and respect for her as a person. *(2 marks)*

10 Read lines 48–53. Explain in your own words the long-term consequences of Pocahontas's death. *(2 marks)*

TOTAL MARKS: 25

Focus on language

Punctuating a list

A simple list will be punctuated by **commas** only. For example,

> The settlers grew maize, fruits, sweet potatoes and tobacco.

In English, the convention is *not* to use a comma before the 'and' that joins the last two items in a list of single words. In American English a comma *is* used before 'and'.

Now, look at the punctuation of the opening sentence of the extract:

> Of the millions of Indians who have ever lived in North America, most people could probably name only three: Hiawatha, the chief who organised the Iroquois into a Federation of Nations; Sitting Bull, who destroyed General Custer and his troops; and a young girl called Pocahontas.

This sentence illustrates how a more complex list should be punctuated. A **colon** introduces the list, expanding on an idea introduced before it. In this case, a statement about three famous Indians is followed after the colon by a list of their names.

In this example, the items in the list are detailed phrases, some of which already contain commas. To make the items in the list stand out, **semi-colons** are used instead of commas between each item, including the last two items.

The **commas** are used to separate the names from the short descriptions.

For practice (1)

Punctuate the following sentences using commas, colons and semicolons where required.

1 Hunger disease mosquitoes and hostile Indians were the main problems faced by the settlers.

2 It was easy to tell each athlete's speciality from his physique the

high jumpers tall slim and ungainly the sprinters stocky well built and muscular and the distance runners light thin and wiry.

3 The marriage of Rolfe and Pocahontas brought security peace growth and stability to the British community.

4 Each rail company has its distinctive livery GNER is classic navy with a horizontal red stripe Virgin red with the Virgin logo in white and Scotrail white with a colourful pattern in terracotta violet and aquamarine.

5 The garden was infested with ants large black fierce-looking ones tiny red ones and white semi-translucent ones.

Looking at the issues

★ Pocahontas came to Britain from an Indian tribe who lived many thousands of miles away. Among the things her husband taught her when she came to Britain were 'customs and manners'. What sort of customs and manners do you think he taught her? What do you think would have seemed most strange to Pocahontas, or been most difficult for her to learn?

★ In 1995, the Disney film studio made a successful cartoon film based on the story of Pocahontas. What aspects of the story do you think are particularly suited to film? (You could think of characters, situations, settings, etc.)

Ideas for writing

★ Write a short story based on the incident when Pocahontas intervened to save John Smith's life.

★ When Pocahontas came to London, she was presented at court as 'Lady Rebecca Rolfe'. She was introduced to the king and queen and all the nobles who attended them at court. Use your imagination to describe the occasion vividly.

Chapter 15

Is There Life Out There?

At a meeting of the Royal Astronomical Society in 2004, it was claimed that our galaxy is full of 'Earth-like' planets which may contain intelligent beings. In the following article, the writer looks at the subject of extra-terrestrial life and the changing opinions of astronomers through the ages.

Extract

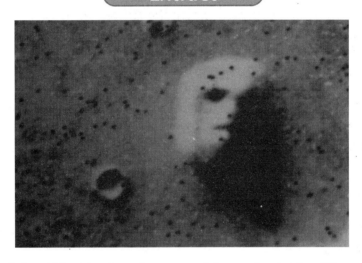

1   One of the oldest and perhaps most important scientific questions is on the verge of being answered. Are we alone in the universe?

Until recently, most astronomers believed that the chances of life, certainly intelligent life, in space were extremely rare. Yet, in
5 less sophisticated times, the early scientists were convinced that we were not alone. More than 400 years ago, an Italian monk called Giordano Bruno wrote: 'In space there are numberless earths circling around other suns which may bear upon them creatures similar to or even superior to those upon our human
10 Earth.' He was burned at the stake for his thoughts.

In the 18th century, a British astronomer, William Herschel, speculated that every planet in our solar system, and even the ➤

sun, was inhabited by intelligent beings. By the 19th century, it became clear that while most of the planets were certainly uninhabitable – Mercury and Venus were too hot, Jupiter and the outer planets too cold – there was one planet that might harbour life.

That planet was Mars. In the late 19th century, the American astronomer Percival Lowell claimed to have observed strange markings on the surface of the Red Planet. He believed they were canals dug by an advanced civilisation to channel water from Mars's polar ice caps to its arid deserts. As a result, the world was gripped by 'Mars fever', with scientific journals full of articles attacking or supporting the idea of life on Mars. Newspapers carried lurid descriptions of what Martians would look like, and H.G. Wells wrote *The War of the Worlds* about an invasion from Mars.

In the years that followed, it became clear that Lowell's Mars was a fantasy. The planet was too cold and did not have enough air to support advanced life. And when the first space probes sent back pictures of a cratered world that looked much like the Moon, all hope of finding little green men – or even little green microbes – vanished.

In 1950, the physicist Enrico Fermi came up with his famous paradox: If our galaxy alone contains one hundred thousand million stars, then at least some of them ought to have planets which are inhabited. If so, he said, where is everybody? More than 50 years on, Fermi's question still holds. Where is all this life and why haven't we heard from it?

Well, maybe earth is unique. Maybe some mysterious factor is needed over and above being the right sort of planet in the right sort of orbit around the right sort of star for life to develop. On the other hand, the universe may be teeming with alien civilisations, who know about us but prefer to keep us in the dark – for the time being at least. Or maybe 'intelligent' life has an unfortunate tendency to self-destruct before it gets a chance to start exploring space properly.

Within a few decades we should know for sure. Telescopes, so powerful that they will not only be able to see distant Earth-like
50 worlds but also even detect life upon them, are now being built. And who knows – perhaps someone out there has already built such a telescope and is watching us right now.

Taking a closer look . . .

1 Read the opening sentence 'One of the oldest …universe.' (lines 1–2)
   a) In your own words, explain the 'important question' raised by the author.   *(1 mark)*
   b) According to the author, how close are scientists to answering the question? QUOTE a few words from this sentence to support your answer.   *(2 marks)*

2 Read paragraph two (lines 3–10). QUOTE a phrase from these lines which means 'in a simpler age'   *(1 mark)*

3 In paragraph two, the author describes the beliefs of two astronomers from the past, Giordano Bruno and William Herschel. Which of the following statements is closest to describing their beliefs:
   a) Bruno and Herschel were totally convinced there was life on other planets.
   b) Bruno and Herschel did not believe there was any life on other planets.
   c) Bruno and Herschel thought that there was a strong possibility there might be life on other planets.   *(1 mark)*

4 Suggest a reason why Giordano Bruno was 'burned at the stake' for his views.   *(2 marks)*

5 Read lines 11–17. Explain the reasons why astronomers in the nineteenth century ruled out the possibility of life on certain planets.   *(2 marks)*

6 Read lines 18–27. In your own words, explain what Percival Lowell believed about the 'strange markings' he had observed on Mars.
                                                                     (2 marks)

7 a) Explain what the author means by 'Mars fever' (line 23), making clear why this metaphor is effective. (2 marks)
  b) In your own words, describe one example of 'Mars fever'. (1 mark)

8 What TWO things which are necessary to sustain life were found to be lacking on Mars? (2 marks)

9 Explain what you imagine by the expression 'a cratered world' (line 31). (2 marks)

10 Consider the writer's tone in the expression: 'all hope of finding little green men – or even little green microbes – vanished' (lines 32–33).
  a) Which of these words best describes his tone: 'disappointed', 'humorous', 'dramatic'? (1 mark)
  b) Explain your choice of answer in a). (2 marks)

11 Read lines 34–39. Do you think Enrico Fermi did or did not believe there was intelligent life on other planets? Explain your answer. (2 marks)

12 In lines 40–47, the writer suggests three reasons why we on Earth have not received any messages from space. In your own words, explain any TWO of these reasons. (2 marks)

TOTAL MARKS: 25

Did you know . . . ?

A **mnemonic** is a device which helps you memorise something easily. Here is a mnemonic to help you remember the order of the planets in our solar system, starting with the planets closest to the sun:

My Very Easy Method Just Speeds Up Naming Planets

The initial letters will give you: Mercury, Venus, Earth, Mars, Jupiter, Saturn, Uranus, Neptune and Pluto.

Can you now see why the popular television show is called *Third Rock from the Sun?*

Focus on Language (1)

Vocabulary

For practice (1)

Find words in the extract 'Is There Life Out There?' that have the following meanings. The words are in the order in which you will find them in the text.

1 put forward as a theory

2 impossible to live in

3 without rainfall

4 horrifying and sensational

5 bacteria

6 an apparent contradiction

7 the only one of its kind

8 swarming/occurring in large numbers

9 destroy oneself

10 periods of ten years

Focus on Language (2)

Structure

A good piece of writing will have a clear structure: that is, the ideas will be deliberately arranged in a particular order. The structure chosen will enable the writer to present his or her ideas more logically, or to present them in a more entertaining or pleasing way.

A writer can choose various ways in which to structure a piece of writing. In the above article, the writer mainly uses **time** as a device to give his work a clearly designed structure.

He begins by making a statement about the position of scientific knowledge in the present; we are told scientists are 'on the verge' of making a discovery.

He then uses a **flashback** to return to the situation in earlier times, beginning his account in the 17th century.

He continues by using a **linear** structure, which means he presents his ideas in **chronological** order (the order in which they happen). He even extends this into the future at the beginning of the last paragraph.

He ends up in his final sentence by returning to the present, where his article began. His piece can therefore be said overall to have a **circular** or **cyclic** structure, a popular pattern to choose as it is satisfying to the reader.

The writer makes this structure clear to the reader by using phrases referring to time, often at the beginning of sentences, such as 'Until recently' (line 3) or 'More than 400 years ago' (line 6).

For practice (2)

Make a list of all the time phrases you find, beginning with these two examples. You should find at least eight more examples.

Until recently (line 3)
More than 400 years ago (line 3)

Looking at the issues

Make notes on the following topics. Then discuss them in groups.

★ *Space travel.* The Americans put the first man on the moon in 1967. Other expeditions to the Moon followed, but public interest declined as the Moon was found to be barren and rather dull. Now, manned flights to Mars are planned for the not too distant future. Do you think the huge cost of this exploration of space is justified? Were the Moon landings a magnificent achievement or a waste of public money?

★ *Meeting up with aliens.* For a time, many people did believe some aliens had landed at Roswell in California, but this turned out to be a hoax. Do you believe there may be life on other planets?

Why are people excited at the idea of finding other civilisations in the universe? What questions would you wish to ask someone from another planet?

Ideas for writing

★ Write a discursive piece of writing arguing for or against the likelihood of there being other civilisations in the universe. (There is a suggested plan for this kind of writing in Chapter Eleven.)

★ Giordano Bruno's crime (offences against religion) was known as heresy in his own time. Imagine you are present at his trial. Describe the scene, and imagine what the prosecution might say, and what the monk might say in his own defence. Alternatively, you could do this task in the form of a play script.

★ Write a short story, or script a scene, in which astronauts arrive at an inhabited planet far into space.